TRANSITIONS FROM VOCATIONAL QUALIFICATIONS TO HIGHER EDUCATION

TRANSITIONS FROM VOCATIONAL QUALIFICATIONS TO HIGHER EDUCATION

Examining Inequalities

EDITED BY

PALLAVI AMITAVA BANERJEE
University of Exeter, UK

DEBRA MYHILL
University of Exeter, UK

United Kingdom – North America – Japan – India – Malaysia – China

Emerald Publishing Limited
Howard House, Wagon Lane, Bingley BD16 1WA, UK

First edition 2019

Copyright © 2019 Editorial Matter and Selection © Pallavi Amitava Banerjee and Debra Myhill, published under exclusive license. Individual chapters © the respective Authors

Reprints and permissions service
Contact: permissions@emeraldinsight.com

No part of this book may be reproduced, stored in a retrieval system, transmitted in any form or by any means electronic, mechanical, photocopying, recording or otherwise without either the prior written permission of the publisher or a licence permitting restricted copying issued in the UK by The Copyright Licensing Agency and in the USA by The Copyright Clearance Center. Any opinions expressed in the chapters are those of the authors. Whilst Emerald makes every effort to ensure the quality and accuracy of its content, Emerald makes no representation implied or otherwise, as to the chapters' suitability and application and disclaims any warranties, express or implied, to their use.

British Library Cataloguing in Publication Data
A catalogue record for this book is available from the British Library

ISBN: 978-1-78756-996-6 (Print)
ISBN: 978-1-78756-995-9 (Online)
ISBN: 978-1-78756-997-3 (Epub)

INVESTOR IN PEOPLE

TRANSITIONS FROM VOCATIONAL QUALIFICATIONS TO HIGHER EDUCATION

Examining Inequalities

EDITED BY

PALLAVI AMITAVA BANERJEE
University of Exeter, UK

DEBRA MYHILL
University of Exeter, UK

United Kingdom – North America – Japan – India – Malaysia – China

Emerald Publishing Limited
Howard House, Wagon Lane, Bingley BD16 1WA, UK

First edition 2019

Copyright © 2019 Editorial Matter and Selection © Pallavi Amitava Banerjee and Debra Myhill, published under exclusive license. Individual chapters © the respective Authors

Reprints and permissions service
Contact: permissions@emeraldinsight.com

No part of this book may be reproduced, stored in a retrieval system, transmitted in any form or by any means electronic, mechanical, photocopying, recording or otherwise without either the prior written permission of the publisher or a licence permitting restricted copying issued in the UK by The Copyright Licensing Agency and in the USA by The Copyright Clearance Center. Any opinions expressed in the chapters are those of the authors. Whilst Emerald makes every effort to ensure the quality and accuracy of its content, Emerald makes no representation implied or otherwise, as to the chapters' suitability and application and disclaims any warranties, express or implied, to their use.

British Library Cataloguing in Publication Data
A catalogue record for this book is available from the British Library

ISBN: 978-1-78756-996-6 (Print)
ISBN: 978-1-78756-995-9 (Online)
ISBN: 978-1-78756-997-3 (Epub)

Contents

List of Figures	*vii*
List of Tables	*ix*
About the Contributors	*xi*
Acknowledgements	*xiii*

Chapter 1   Introduction
Dan Herbert   1

Chapter 2   Vocational Qualifications, University Access and Widening Participation: Setting the Context
Debra Myhill and Sharon Morgan   13

Chapter 3   Statistical Analysis of National Data Sets: Exploring Demographics, Access and Progression of Students in Higher Education from Vocational Entry Routes
Pallavi Amitava Banerjee   39

Chapter 4   Ways of Learning: Student Voices on Learning Experiences across the Transition
Debra Myhill and Sara Venner   59

Chapter 5   Assessment Practices: Student Voices on Their Experiences of Assessment across the Transition
Debra Myhill and Rebecca Morris   79

Chapter 6   Students' Voiced Experiences of Social Transitions: Facilitating a Sense of Belonging
Helen Mackenzie and Rebecca Morris   95

Chapter 7 Lecturer Perspectives on Entry Qualifications and How They Affect Student Progress
Helen Lawson *111*

Chapter 8 Recommendations for Policy and Practice
Helen Lawson *139*

Chapter 9 Conclusion
Mital Kinderkhedia *149*

Glossary *153*

Index *155*

List of Figures

Chapter 1

Figure 1.   Degree Classification by Entry Qualification for 2016–2017 Graduates. 6

Chapter 3

Figure 1.   Undergraduate Students in Higher Education by Qualification Route and Provider. 48

Figure 2.   Students with BTEC Qualifications in Undergraduate Courses. 49

Figure 3.   Degree Outcomes by HE Entry Prior Qualification Route. 51

Figure 4.   Destination of Leavers in Higher Education: BTEC versus Non-BTEC Students. 53

List of Tables

Chapter 1
Table 1.   The Development of VET in the UK.   3

Chapter 8
Table 1.   A Taxonomy of Student Diversity.   147

About the Contributors

Pallavi Amitava Banerjee is a Senior Lecturer in the Graduate School of Education at the University of Exeter. She researches social inequalities of access to higher status universities, and on patterns and processes of progression across the student life cycle and social mobility across multiple generations. She is an accredited Researcher of the Office for National Statistics and a Fellow of the Higher Education Academy, the Royal Society of Biology and the Royal Society of Statistics.

Dan Herbert is Professor of Management Education and Director of Education at Birmingham University's Business School with responsibility for developing high-quality education programmes for the School's undergraduate and postgraduate students. Originally trained as an accountant at the National Audit Office, he has taught in further education as well as at the University of Worcester, Oxford Brookes University and the University of Birmingham.

Mital Kinderkhedia worked as a research associate at Queen Mary University of London (QMUL), joining the last phase of the Transitions Project. Her role involved running focus groups and interview research on the use of Online Modules across the partner institutions. She has an undergraduate in Computer Systems (Thomson Rivers University), Masters in Machine Learning (University College London (UCL)), Masters in Financial Engineering, Birkbeck, MRes in Financial Computing, UCL and is wrapping her PhD in Computational Statistics. She currently works at the Department of Computer Science, University of Oxford.

Helen Lawson is Project Manager and Research Fellow for the Transforming Transitions project. She has over 20 years' experience of conducting research and evaluations, both in this country and overseas, for a variety of organisations including universities, charities, NGOs and community groups. She has also spent a number of years living and working in Latin America and is a fluent Spanish speaker.

Helen Mackenzie is a Research Associate in the Mathematics Education Centre at Loughborough University. She has a MA in Research Methods in Education and her PhD focused upon students' personal experiences of transition within higher education. She is particularly interested in research that examines how different students' transitions might be best supported and enhanced.

Sharon Morgan is an Associate Tutor in Education, and was a Research Fellow on the *Transforming Transitions* project. Her background is as a secondary English teacher, and she completed her doctorate in 2018, researching metalinguistic understanding in writing.

Rebecca Morris is an Assistant Professor in the Centre for Education Studies at the University of Warwick. Her research predominantly focuses on issues relating to current education policy and practice. At present she is working on projects including examining teacher shortage in England, evaluating a new approach to feedback in secondary schools and a review of the evidence on formative assessment in higher education.

Debra Myhill is Professor of Education at the University of Exeter and is the Director of the *Centre for Research in Writing*. Her research interests focus principally on writing, the teaching of writing, being a writer, and the relationship between writing and talk. She has a particular interest in social disadvantage and how literacy can empower and enable both social and academic success.

Sara Venner is an Associate Research Fellow in the Graduate School of Education. A former Primary Teacher and English Lead, her research interests are predominantly around the teaching of grammar and writing in the Primary National Curriculum, and how creative and explicit pedagogies can enable children to make progress in their writing. She is currently studying for an MA in Language and Literacy.

Acknowledgements

We are grateful for the support of the teachers and leaders of the eight institutions who contributed to the project underpinning this book: University of Exeter, University of Birmingham, Loughborough University, Queen Mary University of London, Exeter College, City and Islington College, Leicester College, and Hereford Sixth Form College. Particular thanks go to Professor Tim Quine, Deputy Vice-Chancellor of Education at the University of Exeter for chairing the Steering Group for the project, and for his committed engagement with the project and its outcomes.

We are also very grateful to Pearson, particularly Grace Grima and Hayley Dalton, who were involved in the project from its inception, and provided both venues for meetings, and advice and information on vocational qualifications throughout the project.

Chapter 1

Introduction

Dan Herbert

Vocational Education and Training in Context

In most countries, post-secondary education is, at least in part, split between what may be termed 'academic' and 'vocational' pathways. Academic pathways are most often aimed at preparing students for higher, degree level, education whilst vocational pathways are aimed primarily at preparing students for employment. The status and quality of the vocational pathways vary, with some countries, for example, Germany (Deissinger, 2015), being seen as an example where the vocational and academic pathways have equal status. In others, including the UK, the vocational pathway in post-secondary education has often been viewed as an inferior choice for those not able to pursue further academic study (Unwin, 2004). In the UK, vocational pathways are disproportionately followed by students from low socio-economic backgrounds.

Whatever its perceived status, Vocational Education and Training (VET) is economically valuable and supports the skills needed in society. The Organisation for Economic Co-operation and Development (OECD) identifies short- and long-term benefits from VET for individuals, employers and society. Individuals benefit in the short term from improved employment chances, enhanced earning levels and increased work satisfaction. Employers' short-term benefits include higher productivity from a well-trained workforce and saved costs from recruiting external skilled workers. Society benefits from reduced welfare costs due to higher employment arising from improved transition from education to employment. In the longer term, those undertaking VET tend to access further training later in their careers, employers experience lower staff turnover and society gains from productivity increases and the increased tax revenues this leads to (Hoeckel, 2008).

The provision of VET and the nature of qualifications vary considerably in different countries and contexts. In some countries, such as the Netherlands (MBO, n.d.), the focus is primarily on preparing students for a particular occupation, often linked to an apprenticeship or periods of work experience. VET is delivered in specialist colleges often with a focus on, and strong links with, a particular industrial sector. In others, such as France (MNE, 2010) and the UK, VET also contains a significant proportion of academic general education, and the academic and vocational pathway curricula overlap. Where this is the case, VET may be focussed on career preparation but may also act as a route to higher education. This range of provision means that it is difficult to arrive at a single definition of VET that captures the full range. Moodie (2002, p. 260) suggests that 'one may consider vocational education and training to be the development and application of knowledge and skills for middle-level occupations needed by society from time to time'. Whilst this definition is too general to be applied to specific instances of VET provision, it does capture the key elements. VET is a distinct set of education provision separate to general academic education and provided in ways that support the development of skills, knowledge and behaviours for the labour market.

In almost all countries, a qualifications framework is used to rank VET by level and, in Europe, the European Qualifications Framework (EQF) allows for international comparisons. The EQF allows national qualifications to be compared against set criteria and for VET qualifications to be benchmarked for level against general academic qualifications. In England, Wales and Northern Ireland, the current framework is called the Regulated Qualifications Framework (RQF). The RQF ranks programmes by 'difficulty' and the time taken to study for them. The UK BTEC Extended Diploma qualifications that are the focus of this work are level 3 on the UK national RQF, which equates to level 4 of the EQF. This represents the highest level of qualification below the Bachelor's degree level and the academic A-level qualification is also ranked at level 3 of the RQF.

The Development of Vocational Education in England

The roots of the current English system of VET lie in the late nineteenth century when, in 1867, the Schools' Enquiry Commission identified that a relative lack of technical education compared to other European countries was putting the country at a disadvantage. This related in particular to the technical skills needed for developing manufacturing businesses. In 1875, the City and Guilds of the London Institute for the Advancement of Technical Education was founded, offering a wide variety of courses and examinations in a range of crafts. The development of VET progressed in a haphazard manner with responsibility for VET being seen to lie with employers rather than the state taking responsibility as happened in countries such as Germany (Foreman-Peck, 2004). This situation and the lack of formal structure continued through to the early 1970s.

The origins of the BTEC qualification stem from the formation in 1973 and 1974 of the Technical and Business Education Councils (TEC and BEC). These bodies were formed to provide an improved structure for, and regulation of, VET. The TEC and BEC were merged in 1983 to form BTEC. However, the position of the Council was not secure and in 1994 the development of National Vocational Qualifications (NVQs) as a new VET qualification seemed to threaten other VET qualification frameworks. The NVQ framework was withdrawn in 2015 and since that time BTEC has become a core qualification for 16–19 education.

The BTEC National Extended Diploma is the most significant core level 3 RQF qualification that provides students with a vocational pathway that may lead to employment or university study. It is this qualification which has been the focus of the research underpinning this book. The BTEC Extended Diploma is now recognised as a popular entry route to university, and as can be seen in Table 1, it has equivalence with A-level. In the UK, qualifications acceptable for university entry are awarded tariff points by UCAS. Under this scheme, students achieving the highest D*D*D* grading in a BTEC Extended Diploma achieve the same tariff point score (168) as those achieving 3 A-levels at A*, the highest grade for an A-level (UCAS, 2018). From 2016 onwards, revised BTEC Nationals in 28 subject areas have been introduced, updating and improving the existing qualification. The revised qualification has an increased emphasis on preparing students for further study with improvements to the content and structure of the award as well as revised assessment processes.

Since the 1990s, there has been common political agreement that the status and quality of VET need to be improved if it is to provide the desired outcomes for individuals, businesses and society. A series of reviews and reports have addressed this issue but the VET provision in the UK is still confused and lacking in structure. In 2016/2017 students were enrolled on around 4,700 level 2 and level 3 VET qualifications. The recent political focus on VET has led to a number of reports that investigated the provision of VET. Of these, the Wolf

Table 1. The Development of VET in the UK.

RQF Level		EQF Level	Example Qualification
8		8	Doctoral degree
7		7	Master's degree
6		6	Bachelor's degree
5		5	Higher National Diploma
4			Higher National Certificate
3		4	A-level and BTEC Extended Diploma
2		3	GCSE (Grades A*–C)
1		2	GCSE (Grades D–G)
Entry	E3	1	Skills for Life award
	E2	N/A	
	E1	N/A	

Report (2011) was the most influential and identified significant areas of weakness in VET provision. This report was the most wide-ranging review of VET in England and made recommendations across a range of policy, regulatory and quality issues. Of relevance to the BTEC qualification is the recommendation concerning the nature of qualifications.

> 16–19 year old students pursuing full time courses of study should not follow a programme which is entirely 'occupational', or based solely on courses which directly reflect, and do not go beyond, the content of National Occupational Standards. Their programmes should also include at least one qualification of substantial size (in terms of teaching time) which offers clear potential for progression either in education or into skilled employment.
>
> (Wolf, 2011, p. 14)

The clear recommendation is that VET qualifications should not be purely focussed on preparation for a specific occupational role but should also contain substantial subject content that allows for progression in education, presumably to degree level study, if a student does not move directly into employment.

Perhaps the most significant development in English VET flowing from the recommendations of the Wolf Report is the development of T levels. The first of these new qualifications will launch in 2020 in three subject areas with a further seven areas launching in 2021. T levels will offer an alternative VET pathway for students not wishing to pursue the A-level-based general education pathway in post-secondary education. The objective of T levels is to improve the quality of VET by providing a qualification with general academic content ensuring minimum standards in Mathematics and English, core skills and theory related to an industry sector, specialist skills and knowledge for a specific career and a period of work experience.

In May 2019, a review of Post-18 Education and Funding (the Augar Review) was published. It formed the most comprehensive review of all post-18 education, both vocational and academic, since 2011. The review placed a strong emphasis on the need for improved technical and vocational education. In particular it identified the need for flexibility in entry points, for example, by allowing students with a RQF level 4 qualification to join a degree programme to up-skill or re-skill themselves perhaps after a period away from formal education. The report envisages a regime whereby individuals can access funding based on modules studied rather than whole programmes. Whilst the review focussed on the changes to funding regimes that would be needed to facilitate this flexibility, the proposal poses a pedagogic challenge. How will universities offering more flexible entry routes ensure that students, perhaps predominantly with vocational qualifications, are able to transition effectively back into formal education? The evidence presented in this book regarding the challenges faced by students and the necessary responses by education providers may help inform the design of educational programmes that enable effective transition into education at different stages.

The Augar Review also comments on the structural issues relating to the increasing numbers of students entering degree level education with BTEC qualifications. In particular, it notes the marked increase in students achieving the highest grades in their BTEC studies and the apparent generous treatment of BTEC when allocating UCAS tariff points on which universities make offers to students. The review also comments on the difficulties faced by Further Education Colleges (FEC) which are the main providers of BTEC and other vocational education. The report notes that FECs are subject to a complex regulatory regime, low levels of per-student funding and that staff are paid at levels below equivalent staff in schools and universities. The report's recommendations for FECs relating to funding, investment and regulation present an opportunity for improvements in VET that allow students to be better prepared for further study if they choose to take this route.

The Transforming Transitions Project

The project that forms the basis of this book arose from the need to address the issues that arise when students with BTEC qualifications progress to higher education. The BTEC is a specialist work-related qualification (Pearson, 2018) and whilst it may also provide a route to further study, this is not the sole or primary aim. However, the popularity of the qualification has resulted in increasing numbers of students studying them and also progressing to further study. In 2018, approximately 10% of all university entrants in the UK had studied only for a BTEC qualification. However, this headline figure hides the imbalanced nature of the progression from BTEC to degree level study. BTEC entrants tend to study for a narrow range of degree subjects (Business, Sport and Exercise Science, Health-related professions) at lower entry tariff universities.

The particular issue which provided the impetus for the project was the concern that students with vocational qualifications, such as the BTEC, were not accessing the most selective universities and were not progressing through university in the same way that students with A-levels do. Indeed, the data suggest that the outcomes for students entering University with BTEC qualifications are worrying. BTEC qualified students are less likely to achieve a 'good degree', that is, one awarded at first or upper second class honours using the UK classification system, when compared with A-level students. Higher Education Funding Council for England (HEFCE) data (HEFCE, 2018) show that even those with the best BTEC results on university entry tend to achieve degree outcomes which are in line with those with mid to low A-level results. Figure 1 shows these relationships and that those with the highest ranked BTEC results (D*D*D*) achieve first and upper second class honours awards at a level that compares with those achieving relatively low grade (CCC) A-level equivalents. The pattern is similar for the award of first class honours.

Moreover, aside from eventual degree outcomes, BTEC qualified students are also less likely to complete their studies. Figures for withdrawal from university after one year of study show that BTEC qualified students have higher dropout

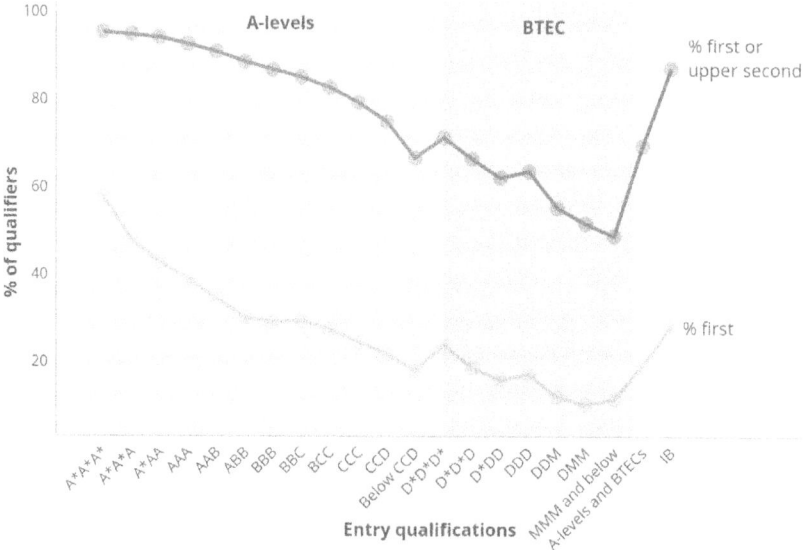

Figure 1. Degree Classification by Entry Qualification for 2016–2017 Graduates.

rates. The evidence shows that BTEC students are more likely to drop out of university when compared with those on a traditional academic pathway, even when accounting for prior attainment (Hayward & Hoelscher, 2011). This emerging pattern of differential outcomes comes in the face of evidence which suggests that young people with more access to the types of programmes and activities (e.g. work experience, career talks, workplace visits and so on) are equipped with better networks and knowledge of labour market and make more informed decisions leading to a more successful transition to adult employment (OECD, 2010; Symonds, Schwartz, & Ferguson, 2011).

The transition to university is an important educational step for students yet the impact of transition experience on final outcomes is poorly understood. There is evidence that personal and academic issues and student expectations that are not addressed during the transition can lead to feelings of estrangement that may contribute to the marked differential outcomes on graduation (Jones, 2018). The Transforming Transitions project was inspired by the desire to better understand the transition journey of BTEC students and to discover whether improving this journey could lead to a closing of the outcome gaps. The project was funded by the HEFCE (now Office for Students) Catalyst programme, Addressing Barriers to Student Success (HEFCE, 2017). This programme was a suite of projects across the country designed to improve the outcomes of students from all backgrounds, and was a response to the earlier work, commissioned by HEFCE, which had highlighted the problem of differential outcomes for students from different groups (Mountford-Zimdars et al., 2015). This had focused on the poorer outcomes for black and minority ethnic (BME) students, students from low socio-economic backgrounds, disabled students and mature students. Our particular interest in vocational education, particularly the BTEC, stemmed from the research which indicated that these students are more likely to be from one or more of these groups, and that the relationship between vocational education, social disadvantage and degree outcomes had not been fully explored.

A key feature of the Transforming Transitions project work was the extent of partnership working between institutions and across the FE/HE divide. Four universities, the University of Exeter, Loughborough University, the University of Birmingham and Queen Mary University of London, and four providers of BTEC qualifications, Hereford Sixth Form College, Exeter College, Loughborough College and City and Islington College, collaborated on the project. This collaboration between universities and BTEC providers was significant in allowing for new insights into the process of transition. Research on student transitions has typically focussed on interventions put in place only once a student has arrived in the new university educational environment (e.g. Leese, 2010). However, transition is a process that starts with the preparation of students for the next stage of their education and this project has specifically explored transition from both the FE and the HE perspectives. In addition, the four universities were all selective, research-intensive institutions because the data show that BTEC students in these universities are less likely to complete than those elsewhere; the salary gap between BTEC students and traditional students, although narrowing, is significant and at its largest in the Russell Group of research intensive universities.

This book considers the potential of BTEC (and other vocational qualifications) as preparation for degree level study. In doing this, we wish to remove the 'deficit-discourse' agenda often linked with VET education pathways, but rather to focus on understanding the challenges faced by students, teaching staff and institutions across the transition. The ongoing discussion around wider and fairer access to university education has centred on looking at defined sub-cohorts of students based on traits such as gender, ethnicity, school, neighbourhood and class (Gorard, Boliver, Siddiqui, & Banerjee, 2019). Too little has been done to relate these issues to the qualifications students undertake prior to joining university. Where this issue has been discussed, evidence that vocational qualifications are not viewed by all universities as an acceptable entry route (Gicheva & Petrie, 2018) has been found, and accusations of 'BTEC snobbery' have been made (Savage, 2018). If ambitions for wider access are to be met, we need to understand and overcome the possible difficulties faced by those joining university with vocational qualifications.

This book, then, studies the vocational pathway to university education from a number of perspectives drawing on both qualitative and quantitative research processes. Through statistical analysis of national datasets, an up-to-date understanding of vocational students' access to and progression through university is offered. Through in-depth interviews with students and teachers in both FE and HE, the views of students and academic staff on practical and academic issues are explored, such as how students adjust to new ways of learning, and wider issues such as the social challenges that face students.

In Chapter 2, we present a detailed overview of recent research which has explored the inequalities of educational outcomes generally, and related to vocational education specifically. The chapter considers perceptions of the value of vocational qualifications, and differential outcomes from university in terms of academic progression, degree outcomes and employment destinations. It also discusses student choices and their learner and social identity and how that might inform our understanding of the differential outcomes for students with a vocational entry qualification.

In Chapter 3, we summarise findings from the analysis of national datasets, government reports and academic literature. We investigate whether students taking up the vocational route have shared characteristics in terms of their background. We also investigate the reasons which motivate students to take up this route instead of the more popular academic routes. We discuss whether cultural capital or vocational habitus may have a role to play. We then follow up entrants in higher education from different qualification routes to see which subjects they study and how their degree outcomes compare. We measure degree outcomes via their results and destination after completion of the undergraduate degree.

The transition from the learning experiences of vocational education to university study may be more difficult than for those from an academic pathway. The skills developed during a vocational programme, such as problem-solving and team-working, are not typically those valued by universities. Universities, especially selective, research-focussed universities, predominantly value academic skills. Chapter 4 presents students' perspectives of the different ways of learning they experience across the FE/HE transition, and highlights both the particular challenges of transitioning into ways of learning at university and how these challenges are frequently shared by students entering with conventional A-level qualifications.

Chapter 5 offers an analysis of students' experience of assessment across the transition, which emerged as a particularly significant concern for them. Typically, vocational programmes use ongoing, coursework-based assessment, sometimes undertaken collaboratively. When they arrive at university they may face an assessment regime that still prioritises the traditional academic essay and examination-based assessment. The dominant culture in universities values independent learning and whilst all students may find this challenging (Spiro, Henderson, & Clifford, 2012), those from vocational pathways may face greater challenges. But the student voices also highlight that for many students, regardless of entry qualification, the shift from very highly supported and focussed assessment practices to more generalised assessment with broader criteria and more limited feedback is a real transition issue.

Whilst students' experiences of learning and assessment across the FE/HE transition are of obvious importance, the students themselves also identified other non-academic challenges as they move from FE into university. In Chapter 6, we share the social issues which students describe, and how those issues can make some students feel they do not belong at university (Rowbottom, 2017). Whilst this is not a problem exclusive to those with vocational qualifications, they may find particular problems experiencing social transitions alongside academic transition, particularly because they are disproportionately representative of socio-economically disadvantaged groups.

To parallel the insights we present which reflect student voices and experiences across the transition, in Chapter 7, we examine the perceptions of educational staff, both in FE and HE, regarding the characteristics and trajectories of vocational students compared with A-level students. The dual nature of vocational qualifications means that students are exposed to learning experiences that prepare them for employment, rather than having a narrow focus on academic development and learning skills. University staff expect these students to be 'practical' and 'hands-on' but these skills may not be valued as highly as academic skills. Implied in some of the responses from teachers in both FE and HE is a deficit model of vocationally educated students.

In the final chapter, we consider the implications of the Transforming Transitions project findings, both for FE and HE, and more widely for educational policy.

Conclusion

This chapter has introduced some of the key themes and contexts this book addresses. It is clear that there are economic and social benefits to be gained from the provision of well-designed vocational education. However, there is a central tension that needs to be addressed. Vocational qualifications in England are designed to prepare students for both skilled employment and as a route to further, university level, study. These students will have skills and knowledge that may differ significantly from those who have followed the academic, general education route – through A-levels or similar. Our universities, especially the selective, research-focussed universities, tend to provide a curriculum that assumes students are joining with the knowledge and skills gained through a general education and not those which are developed on vocational programmes.

We know from research that students from vocational programmes have poorer educational outcomes (Gill & Vidal Rodeiro, 2014) than those from general academic pathways, including higher rates of non-completion and lower degree outcomes. Assuming that it is right for those who can benefit from a university education to be given this opportunity, it is vital that the education system prepare students for this and that universities respond to the needs of students from vocational education to allow them to achieve to their potential. Providing a targeted, evidenced transition from vocational education into university is a key part of delivering this ambition.

The recent changes to VET in England are welcome and provide an improved structure for qualifications. However, for students progressing from BTEC or T levels to university, there remains a fundamental concern. The vocational level 3 qualifications continue to try to serve both students entering employment directly as well as those wishing to progress to university. As such, compromises in the design and nature of these qualifications will be needed. For those progressing to university, it would seem apparent that the providers of level 3 VET, as well as universities who accept these students onto degree programmes, have an obligation to address the attainment gaps that exist for these students. Transition can play a key part in this by ensuring that it equips students with the skills, behaviours and confidence required to succeed. At the same time, the evidence provided in this book signals that many of the transition issues experienced, which may subsequently lead to lesser academic success at university, are not confined to students with vocational entry qualifications but are frequently shared by students from other entry routes and with different social and educational backgrounds. This is where the results of this project have particular value: by adding to our knowledge of transition from school or college to university, through understanding the factors that need to be in place to ensure transition is effective and through identifying the structural factors that hinder good transition practices, there is rich potential to make changes which will not only benefit vocational students but *all* students.

References

Deissinger, T. (2015). The German dual vocational education and training system as 'good practice'? *Local Economy*, *30*(5), 557–567.

Foreman-Peck, James S. (2004). Spontaneous disorder? A very short history of british vocational education and training, 1563–1973. *Policy Futures in Education*, *2*(1), 72–101.

Gicheva, N., & Petrie, K. (2018). *Vocation, vocation, vocation*. Social Market Foundation. Retrieved from http://www.smf.co.uk/wp-content/uploads/2018/01/SMF-Vocation-Vocation-Vocation.pdf

Gill, T., & Vidal Rodeiro, C. L. (2014). *Predictive validity of level 3 qualifications*: Extended Project, Cambridge Pre-U, International Baccalaureate, BTEC Diploma. Cambridge Assessment Research Report. Cambridge, UK: Cambridge Assessment.

Gorard, S., Boliver, V., Siddiqui, N., & Banerjee, P. A. (2019). Which are the most suitable contextual indicators for use in widening participation to HE. *Research Papers in Education*, *34*(1), 99–129.

Hayward, G., & Hoelscher, M. (2011). The use of large-scale administrative data sets to monitor progression from vocational education and training into higher education in the UK: possibilities and methodological challenges. *Research in Comparative and International Education*, *6*(3), 316–329.

HEFCE. (2017). *Addressing barriers to student success*. Retrieved from https://webarchive.nationalarchives.gov.uk/20170712122530/http://www.hefce.ac.uk/sas/barriers/. Accessed on March 21, 2019.

HEFCE. (2018). *Differences in student outcomes*. Retrieved from https://webarchive.nationalarchives.gov.uk/20180405115303/http://www.hefce.ac.uk/pubs/year/2018/201805/

Hoeckel, K. (2008). *Costs and benefits in vocational education and training*. OECD. Retrieved from https://www.oecd.org/education/innovation-education/41538706.pdf

Jones, S. (2018). Expectation vs experience: Might transition gaps predict undergraduate students' outcome gaps? *Journal of Further and Higher Education, 42*(7), 908–921.

Leese, M. (2010). Bridging the gap: Supporting student transitions into higher education. *Journal of Further and Higher Education, 34*(2), 239–251.

MBO (Middelbaar Beroepsonderwijs). (n.d.). *Dutch vocational education and training*. Retrieved from www.mboraad.nl/sites/default/files/publications/brochure_this_is_vet_in_the_netherlands_def_site.pdf. Accessed on May 27, 2019.

Ministere National Education [MNE]. (2010). *National education and vocational education in France*. Retrieved from cache.media.eduscol.education.fr/file/dossiers/61/8/formation_professionnelle_VA_151618.pdf. Accessed on May 27, 2019.

Moodie, G. (2002). Identifying vocational education and training. *Journal of Vocational Education & Training, 54*(2), 249–266.

Mountford-Zimdars, A. K., Sanders, J., Jones, S., Sabri, D., & Moore, J. (2015). *Causes of differences in student outcomes*. London: Higher Education Funding Council for England (HEFCE).

OECD. (2010). Innovative SMEs and entrepreneurship for job creation and growth. *OECD Working Part on SMEs and Entrepreneurship (WPSMEE)*. Retrieved from www.oecd.org/cfe/smes/46404350.pdf

Pearson. (2018). About BTECS. Retrieved from https://qualifications.pearson.com/en/support/support-topics/understanding-our-qualifications/our-qualifications-explained/about-btecs.html. Accessed on April 24, 2019.

Rowbottom, N. (2017). Widening participation and contextual entry policy in accounting and finance. *Accounting Education, 26*(3), 242–264.

Savage, M. (2018). *Top universities accused of BTec snobbery*. Retrieved from https://www.theguardian.com/education/2018/jan/27/universities-btec

Spiro, J., Henderson, J., & Clifford, V. (2012). Independent learning crossing cultures: learning cultures and shifting meanings. *Compare: A Journal of Comparative and International Education, 42*(4), 607–619.

Symonds, W. C., Schwartz, R., & Ferguson, R. F. (2011). *Pathways to prosperity: Meeting the challenge of preparing young Americans for the 21st century*. Cambridge, MA: Pathways to Prosperity Project, Harvard University Graduate School of Education.

UCAS. (2018). *Tariff tables: Tariff points for entry to higher education from 2019*. Retrieved from https://www.ucas.com/file/63541/download?token=uz826-Cb. Accessed on April 17, 2019.

Unwin, L. (2004). Growing beans with Thoreau: Rescuing skills and vocational education from the UK's deficit approach. *Oxford Review of Education, 30*(1), 147–160.

Wolf, A. (2011). *Review of vocational education: The Wolf Report*, Department for Education and Department for Business Innovation and Skills. Retrieved from https://www.gov.uk/government/publications/review-of-vocational-education-the-wolf-report

Chapter 2

Vocational Qualifications, University Access and Widening Participation: Setting the Context

Debra Myhill and Sharon Morgan

Introduction

Recent years have witnessed considerable expansion of the range of post-16 qualifications on offer to school leavers in the United Kingdom (Hayward & Hoelscher, 2011, p. 317), and at the same time, there have been rapid and frequent changes in the nature of qualifications due to changing political mandates. For example, 14–19 diplomas were introduced in 2008 with the intention of bridging the gap between vocational and general education, but were discontinued in 2013 before they had become established. This has created both turbulence for the post-16 and Higher Education sectors, and a complex set of choices for students. A Social Mobility Commission (SMC) report in 2016 suggested that students were faced with 16,000 post-16 qualification choices (2016, p. 116). The sheer volume of choice undoubtedly increases the complexity faced by students and their parents when navigating this qualification system. Whilst on the one hand, choice is often considered to be 'good', and a possible way of increasing engagement at post-16, choice can also render it increasingly difficult for students to convert their qualifications into higher education and economic success (SMC, 2016, p. ix).

Combined with this scenario of complex qualification choices at post-16 is a long-standing concern about who accesses university education and the social and economic benefits it confers. In particular, the fact that middle- and upper-class children have been more likely to attend university than other groups is well-known for over 60 years. Connor et al. (2001, p. 6) note that in 1950, only 3% of young people from the three lowest social groups attended university. Even in the period of mass expansion of Higher Education in the UK, the imbalance in access between working class and middle-class students has remained. Indeed, the analyses of Reay, Ball, and David (2010, p. 467) indicate that the participation rate of the four lowest socio-economic groups actually dropped from 25.61% in 2004 to 24.72% in 2005.

Not all post-16 qualifications are intended as possible routes to university, but there is a range of qualifications viewed as equivalent to the standard route into university via the A-level. These include, for example, the International Baccalaureate, the Cambridge Pre-U, specialist Music and Dance certificates, and BTECs. These different equivalent qualifications are often associated with different social groups or educational backgrounds, and are relevant to the issues of widening participation and differential access to university. The particular focus of the *Transforming Transitions* project has been the BTEC qualification, often described as a vocational qualification. In recent years, there has been substantial growth in the number of students entering university with a BTEC qualification. For example, in the 2015 entry cycle, UCAS (2016) report an increase of 18% from the previous year, and by 50% proportionally since 2011. Students taking a BTEC qualification accounted for 15% of 18-year-old UCAS applicants in this 2015 cycle. This chapter examines the research on the relationship between vocational qualifications and access to university education, and sets out to map the educational terrain in which the Transforming Transitions project has been located.

Words Matter: The Problems of Terminology

One important problem to discuss at the outset here is the linguistic problem of the terminology used in this context. The first relates to the terms we use to describe the differences between social groups. The phrases 'socially disadvantaged' and 'low socio-economic status' are in widespread current use in both research and policy documents. The term 'middle class' is also prevalent, but its parallel 'working class' is far less evident, because of a view that it is now an archaic and demeaning term. Vincent, Braun, and Ball (2008, p. 62) cite the view that to use 'working class' is an 'old-fashioned and, worse, a disrespectful, disreputable phrase, that those who do use it are out-of-touch at best, and at worst, ignorant and prejudiced'. Yet the labelling of people as socially disadvantaged or as low socio-economic status is also problematic as it represents a deficit discourse, defining a group by what they do not have. The term working class can be seen as a positive identity marker, and researchers such as Reay and Vincent have deliberately used 'working class' to avoid 'a denial of working class experiences, based on the false assumption that the viewpoints and perceptions of the middle classes are universal' (Vincent et. al., 2008, p. 63). A similar problem exists in referring to minority groups as 'Black Asian and Minority Ethnic' (BAME), 'Black and Minority Ethnic' (BME) or 'ethnic minority' because they do not fully acknowledge the diversity in these groups. Stevenson, O'Mahony, Khan, Ghaffar, and Stiell (2019) note:

> the problematic nature of using a reductionist term to describe a population that is highly diverse not just in terms of ethnic or racial background but also by dint of socio-economic status, religion and gender amongst others. (2019, p. 45)

In this book, we will reflect the terms as used by authors of the research, but we wish to avoid any valorisation of these choices.

There is also some terminological difficulty in discussing qualifications. There is a strong tendency to discriminate between academic and vocational qualifications, but this is a far from clear-cut distinction. Many so-called academic qualifications at degree level have a highly vocational focus: for example, medicine, nursing, law, accountancy, education and engineering. Again, we will use the terms adopted by the authors.

A final caveat on both these terminological matters is that it is very easy for social grouping distinctions and qualification distinctions to become deficit discourses about particular groups or particular qualifications. It is our intention throughout this book to avoid such deficit discourses, acknowledging diversity rather than deficits. Similarly, it is all too easy to fall into stereotypical presentations of groups which suggest that they are homogenous groups, rather than recognising that all descriptions are generalisations which cannot do full justice to the diversity within these groups.

Perspectives on the Value of Vocational Qualifications

As this chapter focused on the BTEC, usually defined as a vocational qualification, it is important to begin with a consideration of the ways in which vocational qualifications are valued. As a country, we have tended to present rather paradoxical views of vocational education, as simultaneously qualifications which better match young people to the needs of the employment market and as qualifications which are lower status when compared with traditional academic qualifications, such as A-level. Indeed, the Wolf Report, a review of vocational education referred to 'inferior alternative qualifications' (Wolf, 2011, p. 18), and argues that 'academic and vocational education in England have been bedevilled by well-meaning attempts to pretend that everything is worth the same as everything else' (Wolf, 2011, p. 8). Such comments, of course, make no attempt to unpack what is meant by worth, or to consider that there may be differing views about what constitutes worth in this context. BTECs, however, are often considered a valuable qualification for the labour market as they centre on work-based scenarios and workplace skills, such as teamwork: and as Gill and Vidal Rodeiro (2014, p. 6) remind us, 'preparing students for university study is not the BTEC's primary purpose.' As a result of this employment focus, BTECs are often cited as a less appropriate, even 'inferior', qualification as a preparation for studying at university with perhaps more traditional academic learning practices (Gill & Vidal Rodeiro, 2014, p. 10). Several studies conclude that, in the post-16 qualification hierarchy, the traditional A-level rules supreme (Gill, 2018, p. 301, Smith & White, 2015, p. 698). However, the Wolf Report's investigation into the quality of vocational courses indicates that despite Higher Educational Institutions' (HEIs) preferences for A-levels, BTEC National Diplomas are fast becoming a possible route for a wider and more diverse range of students to gain access into HE institutions (Wolf, 2011, p. 33). In fact, in 2015, one in four students entering HE had a BTEC qualification, a figure which has doubled since 2008 (Mian, Richards, & Broughton, 2016, p. 6).

This uncertainty about the value of equivalent vocational qualifications for entry into university becomes interwoven with resistance to the principle of widening participation on the grounds that university is not an appropriate place for mass access. In 2002, at the House of Lords, Baroness Warnock's speech firmly placed her in opposition to the widening of access:

> I believe that, one way or another, we should stop filling our universities with students who displayed no interest in academic matters at school, whose talents are more practical than theoretical, and who will not change [...] too few of them have any interest in continuing to learn. (House of Lords Hansard, 2002)

Implicit in Warnock's assertion here is that vocational equals practical, and academic equals theoretical, and that by implication, university is not a place for those with vocational qualifications. Such a view, of course, vastly oversimplifies practical and theoretical distinctions and the nature of learning in universities: many subjects at degree level involve high levels of practical work – drama, science, engineering, geography, for example. Nonetheless, it reflects the way deficit discourses can easily evolve without any firm evidence base. The same conceptual confusion is evident in the foreword to the Wolf Report, when John Hayes, the then Minister of State for Further Education, Skills and Lifelong Learning, stated that:

> While there have been many calls over the years for greater parity of esteem between academic and vocational qualifications, in practice this has meant making what is practical more academic, to the detriment of both. (Wolf, 2011, p. 7)

Perhaps as a consequence of some of these misunderstandings, a discourse of BTEC inferiority has filtered down into the British media, with headlines such as 'BTECs "set students up for failure" at university' (*The Times*, 2 November 2014) and *The Guardian's* 'Will taking a BTEC help or hinder your university application?' (21 July 2015). Even the online edition of 'Which? University' (September 2016) reinforces this narrative of inadequacy by stating that 'because BTECs are more practical, you don't necessarily get the opportunity to sharpen those more academic skills, like essay-writing, as you would at A-level.' These dominant discourses do firmly position BTECs as an inferior entry route into HE.

The British view of vocational education does seem to stand in contrast to other educational jurisdictions, perhaps most notably, Germany, where vocational and academic education are much more equally valued. In particular, the 'dual system' of their vocational training is much praised internationally for its close partnerships between industry and vocational education institutions. Their vocational system is seen as 'an essential pillar of its economy's competitiveness and capacity for innovation and central to the country's social cohesion' (Federal Ministry for Education and Research, 2015, p. 3).

A very real consequence of this tendency to see vocational qualifications, such as BTEC, as inferior and less valuable than A-levels appears to lead to prejudicial decision-making around entry qualifications. A Russell Group publication (2016–2017), entitled *A Russell Group guide to making decisions about post-16 education*, warns prospective students that following a BTEC pathway might impede their progression into HE: 'However, although BTECs have recently been redesigned it is very important to know that they may not be considered suitable preparation for many Russell Group degree courses', consequently suggesting that BTEC qualifications are 'less valuable than academic qualifications' (Gill, 2018, p. 302). This is an interesting point given the increase in students entering HE via the BTEC pathway. Reay (2001, p. 334) acknowledges this disjunct and argues that 'the contemporary educational system retains remnants of these past elite prejudices'. This assertion correlates with the qualitative findings of Shields and Masardo's (2015, p. 26) study which revealed that during focus group discussions there was a perception among some students that A-level routes were more rigorous than vocational ones. In their study, they refer to a particular student who had a combination of A-level and BTEC qualifications and had selected a Russell Group university as her first choice. In order to gain access into this university, she needed to obtain 280 UCAS points including an A grade in A-level Psychology. However, despite being awarded 400 UCAS points, she was one mark off an A in her A-level Psychology which consequently resulted in her not being able to gain access into her first choice institution. So, despite her high point score (120 points above her offer), she was still denied access.

Differential Access and Participation in Higher Education

As noted in the introduction, the issue of who goes to university and the persistently higher percentages of students from middle- and upper-class backgrounds accessing university education remains a major concern in the UK. The UK has tended to be positioned near the bottom of international measures of social mobility across nations, although this seems to be a problem shared, in part at least, with Australia and the United States. According to Jerrim (2013, p. 20), children from working class parents in these three countries are three times less likely to attend a prestigious university. Reay (2001, p. 334) maintains that educational systems value middle-class cultural capital whilst overlooking working class accomplishments and therefore argues that 'working class relationships to education have always been deeply problematic and emotionally charged, inscribing academic failure rather than success'. Low educational attainment is frequently linked with lower social class status or Black and Minority Ethnic backgrounds, whereas higher attainment is often considered to be a trait of the more affluent middle classes (Greenbank, 2009, p. 83). Greenbank notes that:

> During the past 40 years higher education has moved from an elite to a mass system. Despite this expansion, the working class remain under represented in higher education. They are also disproportionately represented in less prestigious institutions and on lower status courses. (Greenbank, 2009, p. 77)

Crozier, Burke, and Archer (2016) note that although actual numbers of students from widening participation groups have increased, the underlying problem remains:

> In spite of the relative success of the Widening Participation policy and strategies to increase the numbers of students from Black and Minority and White working class backgrounds going to university, universities in Britain continue to be White and middle-class-dominated institutions. (Crozier et al., 2016, p. 39)

Even though there are now more graduates than ever before (Hayward & Hoelscher, 2011, p. 326), universities have made limited progress in terms of widening participation. The 2016 Social Mobility Report, which followed 2010 students transitioning into HE between 2012 and 2014, found that students in receipt of Free School Meals (an indicator for social and economic disadvantage) were 3.6 times less likely to attend a Russell Group university; in fact, this figure rose to six times less likely for students obtaining entrance to Oxbridge (Social Mobility Commission (SMC), 2016, p. 58). For BAME students, the picture is a little different but equally of concern. Although a higher proportion of BAME students access university than white students (Stevenson et al., 2019), they are less likely to attend a Russell Group university, and more likely to attend a local university (Runnymede Trust, 2010). A detailed statistical analysis of entry patterns to university by Noden, Shiner, and Modood (2014) suggests that although BAME students apply in high numbers, their offer rates are lower, and they conclude that:

> the key finding from our analysis, however, is that ethnic and social class differences in offer rates could not be fully explained by differences in academic attainment or patterns of application. (Noden et al., 2014, p. 8)

This concern regarding limited access for these groups of students is echoed in UCAS's end of Cycle Report (2016) in which the Chief Executive, Curnock-Cook confirms that not every child, from every family, is granted equal access to all higher educational environments:

> Young people who come from poor families, or are men, or in the White ethnic group have no less intrinsic potential to benefit from higher education than their peers. And that makes me reflect on the huge waste of potential these current inequalities imply. Of that fifth of the young population with the poorest access to university, just 14,500 go to university each year – only around 6,000 more than a decade ago. (UCAS, 2016, p. 3)

Several studies reveal that similar issues of access present for students with vocational qualifications. In their study into vocational students' transition into HE, Hoelscher, Hayward, Ertl, and Dunbar-Goddet (2008) argue that policy decisions regarding the widening of participation, in particular VET (vocational education and training) courses, do not reflect the reality of what actually happens. They argue that there is an incompatibility between rhetoric in relation to the idea that vocational education may provide an alternative route to higher education. Their study combined 'macro-level' and 'student-level' approaches in order to unearth deeper insight into student subject choices in five HEIs. This exploration involved analysing HESA and UCAS data sets from 2003 to 2004, as well as analysing qualitative data eliciting students' reasons behind these decisions. Their analysis indicated a disparity in the likelihood of attending the more prestigious universities with 13.5% of students with vocational qualifications attending a pre-92 university, compared with 58% of students with conventional academic qualifications (2008, p. 142). They conclude that whilst participation has indeed increased for students with vocational qualifications, inequalities still exist. Their analysis indicates that 'despite the Government claim of "parity of esteem," the traditional A-level route still opens up the best opportunities into those institutions with higher reputations' (2008, p. 149). Similarly, research undertaken by Mian et al. (2016) for the Social Market Foundation study 'Passports to Progress' also found that BTEC students are more likely to go to low-tariff universities than gain entrance into more traditional and elite institutions. In 2015, students with BTEC grades of ABB equivalents or above made up only 2% of students in higher tariff universities (Mian et al., 2016, p. 7). Indeed, it seems the trends identified by these studies is supported by the UCAS data for the 2016 entry cycle which indicates that high tariff institutions accepted only 2.4% of students with a BTEC (UCAS, 2016, p. 25).

These studies, therefore, are pointing to both success and concern in relation to how vocational qualifications increase access to university. On the one hand, it is clear that higher numbers of students are attending university with a vocational entry qualification; but on the other hand, that access is unevenly distributed across the HE sector. The evidence indicates these students are still more likely to attend a lower tariff university than a higher one. Perhaps, as Reay (2001, p. 334) argues:

> within the educational system all the authority remains vested in the middle classes. Not only do they run the system, the system itself is one which valorizes middle – rather than working class cultural capital.

Shields and Masardo (2015, p. 29) point out that whilst there is a disparity between institutions granting access to BTEC students, the greatest polarity exists in research-intensive institutions and there is therefore a concern that the 'marketing of the BTEC, which largely depicts BTEC graduates as succeeding in research-intensive universities' is misleading groups of students who believe this particular vocational route will grant them equal access to all HE institutions – even the research-intensive ones. As a result, they advocate for tighter regulation on BTEC marketing as some promotions claims that BTECs are an acknowledged route into elite universities whilst the actual entrance data for this cohort of students suggests otherwise.

However, there are always dangers in regarding any of these groups – middle class; ethnic minority; those with vocational qualifications – as homogenous groups. Inevitably, there is a high level of intersectionality in these groups. There is a considerable body of data which suggests that students with vocational qualifications, such as the BTEC, are more likely also to be in one or more of the other widening participation groups. Students with vocational qualifications are more likely to be male, have a disability, come from a low socio-economic and non-white background as well as being older than the traditional student (Hayward & Hoelscher, 2011, p. 322). A London Economics report (2013) notes that:

> The analysis of sixteen years of Labour Force Survey data demonstrates that individuals in possession of BTEC Level 3/4 qualifications and a degree tend to achieve their degree qualification at an older age than learners with 'A' Levels; are more likely to have left full time education earlier than their 'A' Level counterparts; and more likely to have experienced a break in their learning. (London Economics, 2013, p. 17)

In their mixed methods study into changing patterns in vocational entry, Shields and Masardo (2015, p. 5) argue that 'students with vocational qualifications are more likely to be from areas with low participation in higher education and demographic groups associated with lower outcomes.' Ethnic minority students, for example, are more likely than their white counterparts to have vocational qualifications (Bhattacharya, Ison, & Blair, 2003). Likewise, Mian et al.'s (2016) analysis found that:

> Between 2008–2015 students entering higher education from the most disadvantaged backgrounds with just A-level qualifications increased by 19%. However, those with BTECs increased by 116%. Those combining both A-levels and BTECs increased by 340%, albeit from a low base. (Mian et al., 2016, p. 6)

The study by Rouncefield-Swales (2014, p. 11) used HESA data to examine trends exhibited by vocational students over a three-year time span. She found that BTEC students were more likely to come from a 'low socio-economic group or a POLAR2 low participation neighbourhood than "traditional entry" students' and less likely to have a parent who had attended university: 42.1% of BTEC students in her study were first-generation HE students, which is 10% higher than traditional students. This then played out into disparities in type of university accessed. During the 2012/2013 entry cycle, '14.5% of "BTEC students" who attended 1994 Group intuitions had a disability [...] compared to only 8.2% of those in Russell Group institutions' (Rouncefield-Swales, 2014, pp. 9–10). She also found that 26.3% of BTEC students entering HE were 'from a non-white ethnic group' compared to 18.3% who entered via the traditional student route (2014, pp. 13–14), and that 32.9% of non-white BTEC entrants studied a Million Plus institution, compared with 17.8% at a Russell Group institution. As a consequence of this pattern, Rouncefield-Swales suggests the vocational pathways are important mechanisms in the widening participation programme as they essentially provide stepping stones for students gaining access into higher education (2014, p. 17), even though there is clearly further work to be done to redress some of the inequalities her study reveals.

As this research suggests that uptake in BTECs is higher among students from underprivileged backgrounds, it may be their post-16 qualification choices are presenting them with potential barriers to selective universities. However, this may be a consequence of limited choice. The 2016 Social Mobility Report (SMC, 2016) argues that one of the reasons for the increase in BTEC uptake from low participation areas is simply because of a lack of access to alternative Further Education (FE) choices. Sometimes this limited choice is geographical in areas where there are few FE institutions. But many of these students also have restricted post-16 options due to lower Key Stage 4 attainment results:

> As with access to different post-16 qualifications, a domino effect of low attainment at primary and then secondary school means that poorer youngsters have fallen behind their peers by 18. However, even when young people from low-income backgrounds do achieve well, they are still less likely to access prestigious universities. (SMC, 2016, p. 103)

Students' post-16 learning experiences are also complicated by wider FE contextual upheavals. FE institutions have faced difficult times of late due to a whole raft of changes: the increase in the participation age at post-16; the rise of institutional accountability measures; the large-scale overhaul of qualifications – all taking place at the same time as funding reductions (Wolf, 2011, p. 8; SMC, 2016, p. 96). However, not all students choose the BTEC pathway as a result of low KS4 results. Shields and Masardo's (2015) study revealed that there were other reasons for choosing this route, which included: lack of A-level subject choice; a desire to attend an FE college rather than stay on in a local 6th form; friendship groups; and family influences (2015, p. 38).

In considering differential access and participation in a university education, the research highlights clearly that those students with vocational qualifications are also likely to be students who would be deemed to have the characteristics of the widening participation target groups. Thus it is critically important not to draw simplistic causal assumptions based on the possession of a vocational qualification, when other factors linked to social class, ethnicity or disability may be equally critical.

Differential Outcomes: Progression and Academic Results

In February 2008, the Select Committee on Public Accounts stated that 'The research-intensive universities that are members of The Russell Group tend to have higher rates of retention than other types of university.' In recent years, several studies have focused on identifying the potential reasons why some universities are more successful than others in terms of retaining their students (Greenbank, 2009; McCoy & Adamson, 2016, p. 168; Reay et al. 2010; SMC, 2016). For example, Greenbank's (2009, p. 93) investigation into widening participation policies revealed that elite universities maintain their status primarily through the admission of higher attaining students as opposed to lower tariff institutions which simply need to recruit enough learners to ensure their economic viability. However, here lies the problem: it is those universities with the highest widening participation success that also have the highest withdrawal rates (McCoy & Adamson, 2016, p. 168; Reay et al., 2010, p. 107; SMC, 2016, p. 105). As a result, it is becoming increasingly apparent that widening participation initiatives need to broaden their focus beyond the initial gaining of access (SMC, 2016, p. 120) to looking more closely at progression, degree outcomes and employment prospects. Indeed, the most recent data from OfS notes that 'we are focusing our efforts here' (OfS, 2019b) as the non-progression gap has changed very little since 2014–2015.

Part of the success of widening participation policies must be to ensure that students are supported throughout their HE journey – not just through the entry process. However, evidence suggests that BTEC students are more likely to drop out of university when compared with those on a traditional academic pathway, even when accounting for prior attainment (Hayward & Hoelscher, 2011; Round, Brownless, & Rout, 2012). BTEC students in Russell Group universities are less likely to complete than those elsewhere. Gauging a deeper understanding of why attrition rates among BTEC students are high is an essential part of the process in ensuring this cohort develop into resilient HE learners and benefit socially and economically from access to university. In her analysis of HESA data, Rouncefield-Swales (2014, p. 19) tracked the patterns of reasons given by students when withdrawing from university — these reasons flag that the retention problem is not simply academic failure, but also more personal and social problems such as financial difficulties, health problems, and employment. Even though overall retention rates have been improving, the 2012/2013 sample examined in this study identified that BTEC students were less likely to complete their HE study compared to A-level students: only 67% BTEC students completed their study compared to 92.3% of traditional A-level students (2014, pp. 19–20). However, she argues that whilst there is a correlation between disadvantaged students and vocational study at post-16, attrition rates are actually linked to *all* disadvantaged students, regardless of their pre-university entry routes (2014, p. 27). A similar point is made by Round et al. (2012) who note that their analysis showed that students with vocational qualifications were also more likely to come from disadvantaged backgrounds. This again is a salient reminder that educational outcomes are attributable to a complex interplay of factors, not simply entry qualification.

However, it is not only attrition rates where differential outcomes are evident. Students' likelihood of achieving a good degree (a first or upper second) differ according to student characteristics. HEFCE's annual reports on degree outcomes between 2013 and 2018 show stable and persistent trends. Students from low participation neighbourhoods are less likely to get a good degree, with a gap varying between 1o and 13 percentage points (HEFCE, 2013, p. 18; HEFCE, 2015a, p. 5; HEFCE, 2018, p. 4). This pattern is true even when prior attainment is taken into account (HEFCE, 2016, p. 3). Similarly, the picture for BAME students shows differential outcomes, though the 2013 report notes some variation here by ethnic group, with black students least likely to achieve a good degree (HEFCE, 2013, p. 18). Both the 2014 and 2015 reports note that white students achieve better degrees than their BAME counterparts, with a steady gap around the 15–20 percentage points mark (HEFCE, 2015a, 2015b, p. 5; HEFCE, 2016, p. 3; HEFCE, 2018, p. 4). The most recent data from the OfS (2019c) indicates that, in 2017–2018, there was a difference of 23.1 percentage points between the proportion of black and white students achieving a First or Upper Second degree. Only the HEFCE, 2013 report looked at vocational qualifications and final degree outcomes and found that these students perform below the sector-adjusted average (HEFCE, 2013, p. 25). Whilst this suite of reports is valuable in drawing attention to differential outcomes according to student characteristics, it is a pity that each of these reports does not look at precisely the same set of characteristics, and there is no analysis of interactions between characteristics.

Given that the under-represented groups at university are also those groups who tend to achieve less well in the school system, it is easy to suggest that the participation problem at university is attributable to lower prior achievement.

However, the relationship between prior attainment and degree outcome presents a very mixed picture. On the one hand, there appears to some clear evidence pointing to a strong association between prior attainment and degree. A HEFCE report (2013), using sector-adjusted averages (allowing for gender, ethnicity, entry qualifications and subject choice) analysed the data from the 2007–2008 entrants to predict the differential degree outcomes between student groups. They found that students from low participation or disadvantaged backgrounds were more likely to do less well than their counterparts from more affluent contexts – even when they entered with the same prior attainment:

> […] only 45 per cent of those in quintile 1 achieved a first or upper second class degree, while 58.6 per cent of those from quintile 5 areas achieved the same classification. (HEFCE, 2013, p. 15)

HEFCE (2016) again reports that students with better A-levels do better in higher education, and similarly, Mountford-Zimdars et al. (2015, p. 10) found that the higher a student's tariff score on entry to university, the more likely they are to obtain higher degree classifications. However, there also analyses, particularly where different group characteristics are taken into account, which suggest this may not be a causal relationship. Jerrim (2013) conducted an analysis which suggested that prior educational achievement explains only 73% of the gap in access to prestigious universities. Both the HEFCE reports for 2014 and 2015 show that more students from state schools achieve a First or Upper Second than those from independent schools, even when they have the same prior attainment (HEFCE, 2015a, 2015b, p. 5; HEFCE, 2016, p. 4). In the light of this, Rowbottom's study (2017) looked at the effect on final attainment of contextual offers, where students from schools in low participation neighbourhoods are given lower entry offers and he concludes that they achieve at least as well as other students. Considering **BAME** students, Stevenson et al. (2019) note that the data shows that even when prior attainment is taken into account, black and Asian students are still less likely to achieve a First or Upper Second degree.

However, these studies and reports have not specifically considered students entering with vocational qualifications, and in general, degree outcomes have been under-researched when compared to other student groups (Gill, 2018, p. 302). One study which did compare the degree outcomes of A-level students compared with those with vocational qualifications identified that, having taken into account the UCAS tariff, A-level students were more likely to achieve a first-class degree (Bailey & Bekhradnia, 2007). Round et al. (2012) found that vocational entrants were less likely to achieve a first or upper second class degree. Likewise, Gill and Vidal Rodeiro's study found that whilst the majority of BTEC students obtained a second class degree only a small number of this cohort gained a first, 'even if they obtained the highest possible grade in the qualification' (2014, p. 6). An alternative perspective is offered by Shields and

Masardo (2015, pp. 5–6) who used mixed-methods which revealed somewhat differing conclusions:

> The quantitative analysis provides evidence that students with vocational qualifications are less likely to receive a first or second-class degree, all else being equal. Yet, the qualitative analysis indicates that students with vocational qualifications are highly capable, and possess qualities of confidence, interpersonal skills and a sense of agency that can help them succeed at the highest levels within the higher education environment. This suggests that universities might better support their learning. (Shields & Masardo, 2015, pp. 5–6)

Gill's more recent study (2018) is significant in that it investigates both degree outcomes in relation to entry qualification and how well different post-16 qualifications prepare students for HE, investigated whether one particular post-16 qualification route was more successful than another. By using logistic regression models to examine the relationship between degree classifications and prior attainment, he found that prior qualifications made little statistical difference in degree outcomes (with the exception of students taking an Extended Project Qualification (EPQ) and Applied A-levels). As a result, he challenges existing evidence which identifies strong correlations between prior attainment and outcomes. He argues that whilst 'purely academic routes appear to provide better preparation for university than purely vocational ones' (Gill, 2018, p. 303), the statistical differences are small, and he concludes that 'all of the various available post-16 qualifications provide a broadly similar level of preparation for university' (Gill, 2018, p. 314).

One interesting strand to Gill's study is his exploration of the data at subject level, and in relation to preparation for university. In terms of subject, he found that when students followed a degree discipline based on the same subject as their BTEC, they obtained better outcomes, and the differences 'suggest that the added advantage of taking a qualification in the same subject area as the degree may be greater for vocational qualifications than for A-levels' (Gill, 2018, p. 315). He notes that:

> [...] the advantage that A-level students had over those taking BTEC Diploma or OCR National Extended Diploma became non-significant when the subject taken was the same as the degree subject, suggesting that for specific subjects these vocational qualifications are just as good as A-levels for preparing students. An interesting area for further research would be identifying in which subjects this is the case, and whether there are some subjects for which vocational qualifications are better preparation. (2018, p. 316)

Gill's study also found a comparative advantage for students who took an EPQ or Applied Levels qualification, and discusses perceptions that these qualifications are better preparation for degree study, and with the EPQ, for example, 'the skills learnt in undertaking this project, such as planning, researching and evaluation, may be similar to those that are useful for degree level study' (2018, p. 303). He also offers the important caveat that this association is not necessarily causal: it may not be the qualification that provides better preparation, but that the students who choose to do these qualifications are already more independent and exploratory. This aspect of Gill's study raises important questions which go beyond oversimplistic generalised data about prior attainment and entry qualification. It begins to explore university progression in terms of specific subjects and in terms of preparation for university. In relation to the latter, it is evident that universities hold perceptions about the relative value of different entry qualifications as university preparation. He notes Russell Group universities advice to potential entrants that some vocational qualifications are 'deemed not to be suitable for some courses', suggesting that vocational qualifications are 'less valuable than academic qualifications' (Gill, 2018, p. 303). At the same time, Gill's analysis indicates that the International Baccalaureate (IB) appears to be no better preparation than other qualifications, despite a widespread perception of its superiority. There are fundamental questions here about whether these, inaccurate, perceptions of the relative value of different qualifications plays out in university admissions processes and in teaching, learning and assessment processes during degree study.

Of course, one complicating factor in all this research relates to whether the current UCAS tariff points which establish attainment parity between qualifications is accurate. Is a BTEC level 3 qualification the same academic attainment as 3 A* at A-level? Subsequently, there is much debate regarding the potential inequity of the UCAS tariff points score and whether in fact the different qualifications have been aligned correctly (Gill, 2015; Gill, 2018; Green & Vignoles, 2012). After all, various qualifications privilege different sets of skills, knowledge and understandings. As a result, this *difference* in terms of post-16 learning trajectories, renders making direct comparisons between students who follow different qualification routes challenging, because 'it relies on the assumption that the points scores allocated to different qualifications are correctly aligned, an assumption which has been questioned in recent years' (Gill, 2018, p. 302).

Differential Outcomes: Employment

The final differential outcome which it is critical to consider is the benefit students derive from their university education. Whilst many benefits of attending university may be hard to measure (such as social confidence; independence; developing a love of learning) one very real benefit is how investment in a university education pays out in terms of employment and financial reward. As with progression and degree outcomes, it seems there is a parallel pattern of lower benefit for the widening participation cohort in terms of employment. The

HEFCE (2013) study found that socially disadvantaged students were less likely to be in employment, and significantly less likely to secure graduate employment than their socially advantaged peers:

> The gap widens again when looking at the percentage of the cohort who achieved a degree and continued to graduate employment or further study, increasing from 41.2 *per cent* for those from a quintile 1 area to 51.8 *per cent* for those from a quintile 5 area. (HEFCE, 2013, p. 16)

A similar picture holds for black students of whom 37.7% gain graduate employment, compared with 48.4% for white students, 53.2% for Chinese students, and 51.1% for Indian students (HEFCE, 2013, p. 19).

This report also looked at the effect of prior qualifications on graduate prospects, and found that the outcome gap between students with post-16 vocational qualifications and those with traditional qualifications increased when examining the differences in 'degree and graduate job or study'. The raw score outcomes (before sector adjustment) indicated that only 38.7% of vocational students were in employment six months after their graduation, compared with 60.6% students with an IB, and 65.5% of students who entered with a UCAS tariff of over 450 points (HEFCE, 2013, p. 24).

However, a London Economics study (commissioned by Pearson) from the same year presents a rather different picture. Using the data collated by the Labour Force Survey between 1996 and 2011, London Economics analysed a range of differential outcomes for students entering with qualifications in BTECs compared to those with A-levels. For this study, they examined students' personal characteristics; the progression rate to undergraduate level; degree outcomes; and students' employment and earnings outcomes. Their findings indicated 'A higher proportion of BTECs plus degree holders are in employment compared to "A" Level plus degree holders (90% vs. 88%)' (London Economics, 2013, p. iii) and assert that whilst they recognise there is a potential difference in graduates' earnings depending on their entry qualification to HE, that this disparity is influenced by other external factors:

> Although individuals with BTECs plus degrees earn approximately 8.3% less per hour compared to individuals in possession of 'A' levels plus degrees, these differences are driven by sector of industrial activity, occupation and especially region of residence. There are a number of regions, occupations and industries where the BTEC degree route offers better earnings compared to the 'A' level degree route. (London Economics, 2013, p. iii)

They conclude that BTEC has an 'employment premium' and that:

> both men and women in possession of BTECs plus degrees are more likely to be employed, and amongst those that are employed, more likely to be employed on a *full-time basis*. (2013, p. 17)

They also note 85% of BTEC plus degree students have become 'managers, senior officials or working as professionals or associate professionals' (2013, p. 18), suggesting that this vocational pathway into HE leads to student success in the workplace.

However, the body of evidence does not seem to concur with this London Economics report. The Social Mobility Commission report (SMC, 2016, p. 91) report argues that whilst BTECs are referred to as being equivalent to A-levels, they do not appear to provide equal measures of opportunities:

> In principle, BTECs are equivalent to A-levels, but they do not offer the same opportunities. Gaining this Level 3 qualification does have higher labour market returns than not doing so, and they can be a route to HE – particularly among young people in low participation areas. However, recent analysis reveals that those with BTECs are most likely to access lower tariff university courses, which lead to lower wages. (SMC, 2016, p. 91)

Consequently the report warns that 'poor careers information, advice and guidance means that bright but poor youngsters are choosing BTECs over A-levels, and so worsening their prospects' (2016, p. 92). This report also identified that students' HE subject choices could impact greatly on their potential earnings. In their study, it was found that certain subjects were more likely to be studied in elite universities and that students obtaining a degree from Oxbridge could have '42 per cent higher starting salaries than degrees from the least prestigious universities' (SMC, 2016, p. 89). They also suggest that degrees in the creative arts had 'been found to give no wage premium over non-graduates in the majority of cases' (SMC, 2016, p. 89). These findings are particularly relevant to vocational students as Hayward and Hoelscher (2011) established that vocational students were 'less likely to study subjects such as medicine, dentistry, law, languages, history and philosophy than those who have taken just general academic qualifications' (2011, p. 322). A more recent study by Belfield, Britton, Buscha, Dearden, Dickson, van der Erve, Sibieta, Vignoles, Walker and Zhu (2018) picks up and confirms several of these themes. The study is an analysis of the comprehensive Longitudinal Educational Outcomes national data set, published annually since 2016. It draws on data extracted from a range of national data sources: the National Pupil Database (NPD); the Individualised Learner Record (ILR); the Higher Education Statistics Agency (HESA); Her Majesty's Revenue and Customs data (HMRC); The National Benefit Database; the Labour Market System; and Juvos, the unemployment research database. The study found, in line with HEFCE and SMC data, that:

> The labour market returns to different degrees vary considerably even after accounting for the considerable differences in student composition. Both the subject of degree and institution attended

make a considerable difference to graduates' earnings. (Belfield et al., 2018, p. 5)

The analysis confirmed the SMC findings that graduates from medicine and law earn more than those from creative arts based subjects, but they also found that the employment dividend for students from lower socio-economic backgrounds with degrees in medicine and law was higher than for their counterparts. Whilst it is not surprising that prestigious vocationally oriented courses such as law and medicine play out into salary advantages, the fact that the dividend is higher for the more disadvantaged is significant. It raises the question of the extent to which vocational qualifications are enabling, or blocking access to these particular degree routes. This report also underlines the effect of university choice on employment outcomes, noting that 'a student may end up with very different earnings as a result of making different decisions about which university to attend and what to study' (Belfield et al., 2018, p. 7).

Student Choices and Social and Learner Identity

Although the choice of which university to attend is only in part a student choice, as university admissions processes will rule out some choices for students, it is nevertheless important to consider why many students with vocational qualifications, along with black students, and those from disadvantaged backgrounds proactively choose not to apply to a prestigious university. Both Archer and Leathwood (2003) and Read, Archer, and Leathwood (2003) suggest that one of the central reasons for non-traditional students application to post-1992 universities is because they feel they are more likely to find people *like themselves* in these institutions. According to Archer and Leathwood (2003, p. 178), lower tariff universities 'were constructed as places offering a chance to "belong," or at least, not stand out'. This same point is made by Thomas (2002) who also refers to the concept of 'belonging' and argues that if higher educational institutions were more 'inclusive and accepting of difference', then students from non-traditional backgrounds would feel a greater sense of belonging, which might result in 'higher levels of persistence' (Thomas, 2002, p. 431). This is particularly true for first-generation HE students who have had little, if any, experience of university life and can therefore feel unfamiliar with their new surroundings, consequently positioning them as an outsider (Archer & Leathwood, 2003, p. 191; Reay, 2001, p. 337). Recent HEFCE research (Mountford-Zimdars et al., 2015), on the causes of differential student outcomes, found similar results which suggest that an institution's inclusivity was central to reducing the barriers which are presented to non-traditional students. This research suggested that further steps should be taken to help maximise student success:

> Positive interventions include creating a sense of belonging, building social capital, enhancing the student experience, and

> developing more wide-ranging learning and teaching initiatives.
> (Mountford-Zimdars et al., 2015, p. iii)

Differences in the nature of social capital that young people bring to their decision-making about university may lead to choices that are less aspirational than they might be. Mazenod et al. (2019) found that student self-confidence was a more significant predictor of university aspirations than prior attainment, which of course, may well be influenced by social capital. They talk about the capacity to aspire and argue that we need to be aware of the variety of factors which interact over time to influence aspirations. Disadvantaged students are also likely to be aware that lower tariff institutions may grant them access than the traditional, research-intensive universities. Few of us enjoy putting ourselves forward into situations where access could be denied (Bourdieu, 1990; Reay, 2004, p. 433). This invisible barrier of being a potential outsider is perhaps less of an issue for students from more affluent backgrounds where there is a taken-for-granted assumption that they will gain access to a selective university (Briggs, Clark, & Hall, 2012, p. 9; Reay et al., 2010, p. 268). Bourdieu (1984, p. 471) implies that having a sense of 'self' can lead us to unconsciously eliminating ourselves from places where we would generally be excluded.

In an attempt to address the 'lacuna' of research centred on working class students' experiences across differing HE institutions, Reay, Crozier, and Clayton (2009), employ Bourdieu's concept of habitus – in particular institutional habitus – to enable them to explore the complex relationship between 'the impact of a cultural group or social class on an individual's behaviour as it is mediated through an organisation' (2009, p. 3). Conceptually, institutional habitus, such as that of a traditional university, is established over a long period of time and is therefore more inflexible in terms of change, less so than an individual's. Reay et al. cite this explanation of the lack of institutional fluidity as one of the potential reasons for non-traditional students' choice of lower tariff institutions:

> Given this and students' dispositions for 'choosing', there is a greater tendency for working class students and students from minority ethnic groups in the UK to go to post-1992 universities, which tend to have more open access and encourage diverse applicants, and for middle-class students to attend pre-1992 universities which tend towards more elitism. (Reay et al., 2009, p. 3)

In this study, researchers tracked the experiences of 27 working class students across four different UK HEIs and explored how the various institutional habitus impacted on their individual learner identities. In their findings, they emphasise the power of each institution's habitus:

> All universities and colleges, including the four in our study, have identifiable institutional habituses in which their organisational culture and ethos is linked to wider socio-economic and educational cultures through processes in which universities and the different student constituencies they recruit mutually shape and reshape each other. In other words the type of higher education institution these working class students attend exerts a powerful influence on how they see themselves and are seen by others in terms of both their learner and class identities. (Reay et al., 2009, p. 5)

In addition to this, the study also found that living at home, as opposed to fully immersing oneself into university life by living on campus or in student halls, restricted the students' development into 'confident academic learners' (Reay et al., 2009, p. 6). Subsequently, they suggest that the process of moving away from home, and from what is familiar, renders students unable to rely on the former structures or relationships in their lives. They have to make new connections. They have to adapt and evolve. Comparatively, the study's findings regarding students attending the more research-intensive universities (which also placed high expectations on learners) suggested that the students had developed stronger learning identities as there was much more pressure on them to adapt and conform to the academic habitus of the institution and consequently students discovered that 'they do academic and do it well' (Reay et al., 2009, p. 11).

Both Briggs et al. (2012) and McCoy and Adamson (2016) argue that institutional support is needed to enable students unfamiliar with the university environment can develop strong learner identities during the transition phrase into undergraduate study. Briggs et al. (2012) advocate for a coordinated partnership between schools, colleges and universities which focuses on creating an opportunity for an HE-learner identity to be formed on the lead-up to HE access (2012, pp. 5–7). Moving away from home and from all that is familiar and being immersed into new academic experiences may aid students' transition into HE and may help create a stronger learner identity. Thomas (2002) found a relative disadvantage for students who do not live in student accommodation research echoes this as she found that they were 'more likely to feel marginalised from their peers, and thus that they occupy a lower position' (2002, p. 436). The re-negotiating of a new identity is central to the multiple ways in which working class students access and work within educational institutions (Archer & Leathwood, 2003, p. 175). In terms of the need to have adaptive identities, the philosopher Bauman (2004), reminds us that only having one identity can be problematic: 'In our fluid world, committing oneself to a single identity for life, or even for less than a whole life but for a very long time to come, is a risky business' (2004, p. 84). It may be that the more traditional student, with advantageous social capital, has already acquired a more flexible, multiple identity, which supports their transition into an academic environment. As Bourdieu (1990) maintains, the middle classes 'move in their world as a fish in water' (1990, p. 163). There is comparatively less need for a middle-class student to change their language, tastes or their identity when attending HE institutions. They are on the *inside*, therefore, placing non-traditional students as *the Other*. Vocational students, on the other hand, may face some degree of difficulty when accessing the potentially unfamiliar and academic language associated with HE learning, which in turn might lead to increasing feelings of alienation and isolation. As McArthur (2011, p. 736) states:

> Higher education should enable students to develop and celebrate their own identities. To do that, students need to be able to develop their own voices in ways that enrich rather than suppress who they are.

Conclusion

This chapter has outlined the most pertinent issues related to vocational qualifications, particularly the BTEC, and has shown that several studies are pointing to concerns about differential outcomes for BTEC students. They are: less likely to go to university; less likely to go to a Russell Group university; more likely not to complete their degrees; less likely to achieve a first or upper second class degree; and less likely to secure graduate employment. Put like this, it is a rather bleak picture. But the chapter has also demonstrated that the cohort of students who take vocational qualifications are also more likely to share characteristics of the widening participation cohort, particularly in terms of social disadvantage and ethnicity. The OfS latest report on disparities in educational progression and outcomes for disadvantaged students echoes strongly the pattern found for BTEC students:

> For each stage of the student lifecycle (access, continuation, attainment, progression) at each university, college and other higher education provider on the OfS Register, the data set shows gaps between:
>
> - students from the most and least advantaged areas (POLAR quintiles 5 and 1);
> - white and black, Asian and minority ethnic students;
> - young (under 21 on entry) and mature (21 and over on entry) students;
> - disabled and non-disabled students;
> - male and female students;
> - students who were eligible for free school meals and those who were not.
>
> OfS (2019a)

The chapter has also highlighted some conflicting findings, particularly around the effects of prior attainment on degree outcome, and the inconsistent nature of national reporting. Prior qualification is not yet routinely used in these analyses, despite the recommendation of Shields and Masardo (2015) that 'students with vocational qualifications should be added to the demographic groups for which BIS [Department for Business and Industry] monitors retention and success' (2015, p. 6). As a consequence, it is also likely that neither schools nor universities are alert to the possible different outcomes for their students with vocational qualifications. Similarly, there is an urgent need for analyses that looks more closely at interactions *between* characteristics or groups, so that we can better 'understand the intersectionality of different student characteristics and their link with progression and attainment outcomes' (Mountford-Zimdars et al., 2015, p. 96). This also avoids the risk of generating claims which treat students with vocational qualifications (and indeed students in other disadvantaged groups) as homogenous, when they are heterogeneous and diverse.

It is also the case that the growing numbers of students entering university through the BTEC entry route has successfully ensured that university education is not only a possibility for the privileged, but is a realistic opportunity for the disadvantaged. It provides students with a stepping stone into higher education (Rouncefield-Swales, 2014), and many succeed. It is important to remember that despite the differential outcomes described here, the majority of students with vocational qualifications do succeed at university, and it is important to eschew deficit discourses of this group of students, or indeed of any the groups of students discussed in this chapter. However, the predicted number of students wishing to access university education is set to increase by 23% after 2019 (Bekhradnia & Beech, 2018, p. 4), at the same time as university funding through fees is likely to decrease. As a consequence of this, it is possible that in a market which can be selective, particularly for the Russell Group universities, admissions decisions favour the traditional A-level entry students.

The issues discussed in the chapter also raise larger, more systemic questions for universities and schools to consider and address. The persistent patterns of differential outcomes for students who are not part of the traditional white, middle-class entry cohort should stand as a warning against curriculum, teaching and learning experiences which are ideally suited to the dominant group but do not recognise the needs, interests and aptitudes of a diverse learning community. McArthur (2011) argues persuasively for the need for universities to diversify their intake within a vision for higher education as pluralist and inclusive:

> The sounds of higher education should therefore be a cacophony of different voices. There should be shouting. Higher education should challenge, provoke and inspire. It should look messy. It should not fit neatly within the lines of an accountant's ledger.

> It should look rather like the world in which it exists and which it partly serves. (McArthur, 2011, p. 737)

Even though there is clearly *difference* in all student groups transitioning into higher education, it appears that some groups are more different than others and are therefore automatically positioned as outsiders in the domains of traditional educational institutions. Whilst, as much of the recent research suggests, quantitative studies inform us of statistical differences, further qualitative research is needed in order for these 'different voices' to be fully heard. As Biesta (2006, p. 178) argues, 'Democracy, in its shortest formula, is about learning from difference and learning to live with others who are not like us.' Clearly, if government intention is to ensure that *all* students are given equal access to *all* higher educational institutions as well as the experience of degree success and graduate employment, widening participation initiatives need to move beyond the entry process and to think more critically about the full university experience. Acknowledging difference and promoting inclusivity will inevitably require universities to change conservative ways of thinking about teaching and learning, and to recognise the benefit a more diverse learning community offers for *all* learners in it. At the same time, universities cannot solve this problem on their own. Too many students are, in effect, excluded from access to university by low attainment, or unwise subject or qualification choices. It remains critically important that schools and FE colleges have high expectations of all students, and continue to seek to close the gap in attainment at school between the advantaged and the disadvantaged, as some schools have already powerfully demonstrated. In response to the findings of 2016 UCAS report, UCAS Chief Executive, Mary Curnock Cook (UCAS, 2016, p. 4) argued that change needs to take place much earlier in a student's educational journey and that:

> This suggests a major collaborative initiative across multiple phases of education, implying a decade or more before we start seeing significant results. But with the new story told by the data in this report, I believe it is one that should start now. (UCAS, 2016, p. 4)

Such collaboration will require deep partnerships across key educational boundaries, with particular consideration of the principal educational transition points, and how those transitions can be made less difficult for students.

For many people, education is a mechanism which opens doors: both in terms of personal enlightenment as well as through educational and economic success. But what has become evident is that we are not all afforded the same opportunities which enable us to make the same choices in life. As Bauman (1998) says, 'All of us are doomed to the life of choices, but not all of us have the means to be choosers' (1998, p. 86). What is needed is widening participation with a commitment to equality of outcomes, and the assurance that all students, regardless of social background, are also provided with the opportunity to be 'choosers'.

References

Archer, L., & Leathwood, C. (2003). Identities, inequalities and higher education. In Archer, L., Hutchings, M., & Ross (Eds.), *A higher education and social class: Issues of exclusion and inclusion* (pp. 175–192). Oxford: RoutledgeFalmer.

Bailey, N., & Bekhradnia, B. (2007). *The academic experience and outcomes of students with vocational level 3 qualifications*. Oxford: HEPI.

Bauman, Z. (1998). *Globalization: human consequences*. Cambridge: Polity Press.

Bauman, Z. (2004). *Identity: Conversations with Benedetto Vecchi*. Cambridge: Polity Press.

Bekhradnia, B., & Beech, D. (2018). Demand for higher education to 2030. *HEPI Report 105: HEPI*. Retrieved from www.hepi.ac.uk/wp-content/uploads/2018/03/HEPI-Demand-for-Higher-Education-to-2030-Report-105-FINAL.pdf

Belfield, C., Britton, J., Buscha, F., Dearden, L., Dickson, M., van der Erve, L., ... Zhu, Y. (2018). *The relative labour market returns to different degrees*. London: Institute for Fiscal Studies. Retrieved from https://www.ifs.org.uk/publications/13036

Bhattacharya, G., Ison, L., & Blair, M. (2003). *Minority ethnic attainment and participation in education and training: The evidence*. DfES Research Topic Paper RTP01-03. DfES, London.

Biesta, G. J. J. (2006). What's the point of lifelong learning if lifelong learning has no point? On the democratic deficit of policies for lifelong learning. *European Educational Research Journal, 5*(3–4), 169–180.

Bourdieu, P. (1984). *Distinction: A social critique of the judgement of taste*. London: Routledge.

Bourdieu, P. (1990). *The logic of practice*. R. Nice (Trans.), Stanford, CA: Stanford University Press.

Briggs, A. R. J., Clark, J., & Hall, I. (2012). Building bridges: Understanding student transition to University. *Quality in Higher Education, 18*(1), 3–21.

Connor, H., Dewson, S., Ters, C., Eccles, J., Regan, J., & Aston, J. (2001). *Social class and higher education: Issues affecting decisions on participation by lower social class groups*. London: Institute for Employment Studies.

Crozier, G., Burke, P. J., & Archer, L. (2016). Peer relations in higher education: Raced, classed and gendered constructions and othering. *Whiteness and Education, 1*(1), 39–53.

Federal Ministry of Education and Research. (2015). Report on Vocational education and Training 2015. Retrieved from https://www.bmbf.de/upload_filestore/pub/Berufsbildungsbericht_2015_eng.pdf

Gill, T. (2015). Using generalised boosting models to evaluate the UCAS tariff. *Research Matters: A Cambridge Assessment Publication, 20*, 2–6.

Gill, T. (2018). Preparing students for university study: A statistical comparison of different post-16 qualifications. *Research Papers in Education, 33*(3), 301–319.

Gill, T., & Vidal Rodeiro, C. L. (2014). *Predictive validity of level 3 qualifications: Extended project, Cambridge Pre-U, International Baccalaureate, BTEC Diploma*. Cambridge Assessment Research Report. Cambridge, UK: Cambridge Assessment.

Green, F., & Vignoles, A. (2012). An empirical method for deriving grade equivalence for university entrance qualifications: An application to A-levels and the International Baccalaureate. *Oxford Review of Education, 38*(4), 473–491.

Greenbank, P. (2009). *Widening participation and social class*. Retrieved from https://www.researchgate.net/publication/273768422_Widening_participation_and_social_class. Accessed on April 4, 2017.

Hayward, G., & Hoelscher, M. (2011). The use of large-scale administrative data sets to monitor progression from vocational education and training into higher education in the UK: Possibilities and methodological challenges. *Research in Comparative and International Education, 6*(3), 316–329.

HEFCE. (2013). *Higher education and beyond: Outcomes from full-time first degree study*. Retrieved from http://www.hefce.ac.uk/pubs/year/2013/201315/. Accessed on May 21, 2017.

HEFCE. (2015a). *Differences in employment outcomes: Equality and diversity characteristics*. Retrieved from http://www.hefce.ac.uk/pubs/year/2015/201523/. Accessed on May 21, 2017.

HEFCE. (2015b). *Causes of differences in student outcomes*. Retrieved from http://www.hefce.ac.uk/pubs/rereports/Year/2015/diffout/. Accessed on May 21, 2017.

HEFCE. (2016). *Higher education in England 2016: Key facts*. Retrieved from http://www.hefce.ac.uk/pubs/year/2016/201620/. Accessed on May 21, 2017.

HEFCE. (2018). *Differences in student outcomes*. Retrieved from https://webarchive.nationalarchives.gov.uk/20180405115303/http://www.hefce.ac.uk/pubs/year/2018/201805/

Hoelscher, M., Hayward, G., Ertl, H., & Dunbar-Goddet, H. (2008). The transition from vocational education and training to higher education: A successful pathway? *Research Papers in Education, 23*(2), 139–151.

House of Lords Hansard. (2002). University Finance Debate: Baroness Warnock 641 (9), November 27, 2002. Retrieved from https://publications.parliament.uk/pa/ld200203/ldhansrd/vo021127/text/21127-07.htm#column_794. Accessed on August 4, 2019.

Jerrim, J. (2013). *Family background and access to 'high status' universities*. London: The Sutton Trust.

London Economics. (2013). *The outcomes associated with the BTEC route of degree level acquisition: A report for Pearson*. London Economics: London. Retrieved from https://londoneconomics.co.uk/blog/publication/the-outcomes-associated-with-the-btec-route-of-degree-level-acquisition/. Accessed on May 21, 2017.

Mazenod, A., Francis, R., Archer, L., Hodgen, A., Taylor, R., Tereshchenko, A., … Pepper, D. (2019). Nurturing learning or encouraging dependency? Teacher constructions of students in lower attainment groups in English secondary schools. *Cambridge Journal of Education, 49*(1), 53–68.

McArthur, J. (2011). Reconsidering the economic and social purposes of higher education. *Higher Education Research and Development, 30*(6), 737–749. doi:10.1080/07294360.2010.539596

McCoy, T., & Adamson, D. (2016). Building a house on sand? In: G. Steventon, D. Cureton, & L. Clouder (Eds.), *Student attainment in higher education: Issues, controversies and debates*. Oxford: Routledge. 161–173.

Mian, E., Richards, B., & Broughton, N. (2016). *Passports to progress*. London: Social Market Foundation.

Mountford-Zimdars, A., Sabri, D., Moore, J., Sanders, J., Jones, S., & Higham, L. (2015). *Causes of differences in student outcomes*. London: HEFCE.
Noden, P., Shiner, M., & Modood, T. (2014). *Black and minority ethnic access to higher education a reassessment* Nuffield/LSE. Retrieved from www.lse.ac.uk/website-archive/newsAndMedia/PDF/NuffieldBriefing.pdf
OfS. (2019a). *New data reveals university performance on access and student success*. Retrieved from www.officeforstudents.org.uk/news-blog-and-events/press-and-media/new-data-reveals-university-performance-on-access-and-student-success/. Accessed on March 2, 19.
OfS. (2019b). *Official statistic: Key performance measure 3*. Retrieved from www.officeforstudents.org.uk/about/measures-of-our-success/participation-performance-measures/gap-in-non-continuation-between-most-and-least-represented-groups/. Accessed on March 2, 19.
OfS. (2019c). *Official statistic: Key performance measure 4*. Retrieved from www.officeforstudents.org.uk/about/measures-of-our-success/participation-performance-measures/gap-in-degree-outcomes-1sts-or-21s-between-white-students-and-black-students/ Accessed on March 2, 19.
Read, B., Archer, L., & Leathwood, C. (2003). Challenging cultures? Student conceptions of 'belonging' and 'isolation' at a post-1992 university. *Studies in Higher Education*, *28*(3), 261−277.
Reay, D., (2001). Finding or losing yourself?: Working-class relationships to education. *Journal of Education Policy*, *16*, 333−346. doi:10.1080/02680930117164
Reay, D., (2004). 'It's all becoming a habitus': Beyond the habitual use of habitus in educational research. *British Journal of Sociology of Education*, *25*(4), 431−444.
Reay, D., Ball, S., & David, M. (2010). 'It's taking me a long time but I'll get there in the end': Mature students on access courses and higher education choice. *British Education Research Journal*, *28*(1), 5−19.
Reay, D., Crozier, G., & Clayton, J. (2009). 'Fitting in' or 'standing out': Working-class students in UK higher education. *British Educational Research Journal*, *36*(1), 107−124.
Rouncefield-Swales, A. (2014). *Vocational progression to selecting universities comparisons and trends 2010−2013*. Retrieved from http://www.careerpilot.org.uk/upload/Final_BTEC_Research_2014.pdf. Accessed on April 4, 2017.
Round, D., Brownless, C., & Rout, A. (2012). The landscape of vocational progression in higher education: Understanding the retention and progression of vocational learners through a regional perspective. *Research in Post-Compulsory Education*, *17*(1), 5−19.
Rowbottom, N. (2017). Widening participation and contextual entry policy in accounting and finance. *Accounting Education*, *26*(3), 242−264.
Runnymede. (2010). *Ethnicity and participation in education*. London: Runnymede Trust. Retrieved from www.runnymedetrust.org/uploads/Parliamentary%20briefings/HigherEducationNovember2010.pdf. Accessed on January 1, 2019.
Russell Group. (2016−17). *Informed choices: A Russell group guide to making decisions about post-16 education*. London: Russell Group.
Shields, R., & Masardo, A. (2015). *Higher education in England 2016: Key facts*. New York, NY: Higher Education Academy. Retrieved from https://www.heacademy.ac.uk/knowledge-hub/changing-patterns-vocational-entry-qualifications-student-support-and-outcomes. Accessed on May 21, 2017.

Smith, E., & White, P. (2015). What makes a successful undergraduate? The relationship between student characteristics, degree subject and academic success at university. *British Educational Research Journal, 41*(4), 686–708.

Social Mobility Commission. (2016). *State of the nation 2016: Social mobility in great Britain*. London: Social Mobility Commission. Retrieved from https://www.gov.uk/government/uploads/system/uploads/attachment_data/file/569410/Social_Mobility_Commission_2016_REPORT_WEB__1__.pdf. Accessed on April 4, 2017.

Stevenson, J., O'Mahony, J., Khan, O., Ghaffar, F., & Stiell, B. (2019). *Understanding and overcoming the challenges of targeting students from under-represented and disadvantaged ethnic backgrounds*. Retrieved from www.officeforstudents.org.uk/media/d21cb263-526d-401c-bc74-299c748e9ecd/ethnicity-targeting-research-report.pdf. Accessed on March 18, 2019.

Thomas, L. (2002). Student retention in higher education: The role of institutional habitus. *Journal of Education Policy, 17*(4), 423–442.

UCAS. (2016). *End of cycle report 2016: UCAS analysis and research*. Cheltenham: UCAS. Retrieved from https://www.ucas.com/file/86541/download?token=PQnaAI5f. Accessed on May 13, 2017.

Vincent, C., Braun, A., & Ball, S. J. (2008). Childcare, choice and social class: Caring for young children in the UK. *Critical Social Policy, 28*(1), 5–26.

Wolf, A. (2011). *Review of vocational education*. The Wolf Report. Retrieved from https://www.gov.uk/government/publications/review-of-vocational-education-the-wolf-report. Accessed on June 21, 2019.

Chapter 3

Statistical Analysis of National Data Sets: Exploring Demographics, Access and Progression of Students in Higher Education from Vocational Entry Routes

Pallavi Amitava Banerjee

Introduction

In this chapter, we investigate which students take up vocational routes, for example, to explore if there are there any background characteristics which are common among these group of students and to determine what factors seem to be driving these choices. The chapter then considers the access, attainment, continuation and progression of these students in undergraduate courses and compare it with their peers from other entry qualification routes. Finally, we investigate the degree outcomes of these students, both in terms of qualification outcomes and their employment routes. The two measures used to interrogate this are: achieving a suitable qualification at the end of the course; and the destination of leavers, whether they are in further education, employment, training, or looking for work. We do this by making use of official data sets available from the Department for Education (DfE) and the Higher Education Statistics Agency (HESA).

The chapter presents a diverse suite of analyses to help understand the ways in which students with vocational qualifications access and progress through university. Government statistics are analysed to indicate whether students taking up the vocational route are lower achievers and/or from a particular background. This analysis is then discussed in the context of the research addressing this, and considered alongside the information available from policy documents to understand why students choose this qualification route. We also assess whether there are any particular demographic characteristics shared among these students to ascertain whether certain social groups who may share a vocational habitus are predisposed to taking up this qualification route rather than others. We do this by retrospectively tracking prior attainment in school for students taking the vocational course. At the age of 16, most students in England take standardised national tests, the General Certificate of Secondary Education (GCSEs). The GCSE results of students who take up the vocational route are compared with those who take up more academically focussed qualification routes.

A comprehensive analysis of longitudinal data for UK domiciled first-year students has allowed us to understand vocational routes through university. We follow through the cohort of students who had enroled for full-time study for their first degree at a higher education provider in England during the academic year 2012–2013, and track their progress via attainment and destination data. This mapping activity enables us to see whether the students from this cohort were more likely to have completed their three- or four-year undergraduate courses, or to be in employment, further education, training or drop out of the course, or to be unemployed. These are only some of the possibilities and, as the chapter will illustrate, there were several other trajectories for the students to pursue. The analysis has also looked at students who had studied vocational qualifications such as BTECs, either as stand-alone qualifications, or in combination with other qualifications. We then compare attainment and destination data of BTEC students with that of non-BTEC students who take up academically focused qualification routes such as the A-levels or International Baccalaureate (IB).

The Social Context

The link between various indices of deprivation and the student life-cycle can be extended further to explore the connections with intergenerational social mobility. There is a growing national concern about the relative underperformance of students from disadvantaged social backgrounds (HEPI, 2019; SMC, 2016, 2019). Low educational attainment is frequently linked with lower socioeconomic status, whereas higher attainment is often linked to students from affluent middle classes (Greenbank, 2009, p. 83; Thompson, 2014). Notably, as working class students have weaker academic outcomes, they end up in jobs held in lower esteem and are deemed to have inferior labour market outcomes (Crawford, 2014). This relationship has important implications for intergenerational mobility, and to ensure equality of opportunity (Thompson, 2014) and provide a second chance, several measures are being taken at the local, regional and national level. The government acknowledges the relationship between social and educational disadvantage and aims to double university places for students from low participation areas (SMC, 2016, p. 115). Notably, the regulator for higher education access and participation – the newly formed Office for Students (OfS) – also considers supporting disadvantaged students to be an area of priority. Several criteria are used in the UK to mark deprivation such as area of residence, family income, being first in the family to go to a university, and children who are young carers or have been looked after.

Examination of inequalities between groups of students taking different pre-university qualification routes has revealed that students who do not take conventional academic pathways are more likely to be from areas with low participation in higher education and demographic groups associated with lower outcomes (Shields & Masardo, 2015). It is worth mentioning here that areas with lower participation rates in higher education are identified by the post code where a student lives. The Participation of Local Areas (POLAR) terminology was introduced by the Higher Education Funding Council of England (HEFCE). Analysing the likelihood of young people aged 18–19 entering higher education, it classifies local areas in the UK into five quintiles where quintile one has the lowest participation rate and quintile five has the highest. A more recent study has reinforced these findings by making use of HESA data, where they examine trends exhibited by vocational students over three years (Rouncefield-Swales, 2014). Reportedly, BTEC students are more likely to come from a lower socio-economic class or live in a low participation neighbourhood than traditional entry students. 42.1% of BTEC students in the data were first generation HE students − which is 10% higher than traditional students (Rouncefield-Swales, 2014, p. 11).

Inequalities during the life course are being by addressed by the government, not just by widening access but also by offering support in HE. This is because one of the major problems faced by the HE sector is that of attrition and decisively disadvantaged students are more likely to drop out from their courses. Increasing the chances of these students in completing a higher education degree is a step closer to equity. Apparently, universities with the highest widening participation success rates also have the highest withdrawal rates (McCoy & Adamson, 2016, p. 168; Reay, Crozier, & Clayton, 2009, p. 107; SMC, 2016, p. 105). As a result, it is becoming increasingly clear that widening participation initiatives need to broaden their focus beyond the initial gaining of access (SMC, 2016, p. 120), particularly as it is suggested that students from disadvantaged backgrounds are more likely to drop out or obtain lower degree classifications than their peers (McCoy & Adamson, 2016, p. 168; SMC, 2016, p. 105).

Critics often question whether higher education is really the passport to social mobility. Nevertheless, irrespective of the learner's identity, it is important to ensure that students are supported throughout their HE journeys − not just through the entry process − in order to help the widening participation agenda, succeed. It is also important to understand why attrition rates among students from certain social groups are higher in the first place. Once the reasons are understood only then can measures be taken to ensure these students develop into resilient and successful learners. For example, when a student submits an intention to leave the course or university, they are asked to provide the reason for withdrawal. This data can be tracked via HESA data and reveals that the main reasons for withdrawal are linked to academic failure, finance, health, and employment. Even though overall retention rates have been improving, the 2012/3 data shows that BTEC students were less likely to complete their HE study compared to A-level students: only 67% BTEC students completed their study compared to 92.3% of A-level students (Rouncefield-Swales, 2014, pp. 19–20). However, whilst there is a correlation between disadvantaged students and vocational study at post-16, attrition rates are actually linked to *all* disadvantaged students, regardless of their pre-university entry routes (Rouncefield-Swales, 2014, p. 27).

Prior education in terms of the actual attainment score (entry tariff), as well as the qualification route taken, plays an important role in deciding whether students are viewed favourably by universities during admissions decision-making. Widening access and supported progression measures therefore need an accurate prediction of potential attainment at HE (Gill & Vidal Rodeiro, 2014, p. 4). For example, HE entrants take various prior qualification routes but it remains unclear and debatable whether all these different qualifications have been aligned correctly (Gill, 2017; Green & Vignoles, 2012). The different qualifications via their different curriculum, pedagogical approach and course work bestow students with different sets of skills, knowledge and understanding. As a result, this *difference* in terms of post-16 learning trajectories renders making direct comparisons between students who follow different qualification routes complex (Gill, 2017, p. 11). As the earlier chapter has shown, vocational entry route students have a unique skill set and strengths, as do students who come from academic qualification routes. While these may not necessarily be harnessed in HE, these are surely transferable skills which can be beneficial to learners in the long run.

As was noted in the previous chapter, the majority of BTEC students obtain a second-class degree and only a small number of this cohort gain a first, even if they had obtained the highest possible grade in the vocational qualification (Gill & Vidal Rodeiro, 2014). The reports present a deficit model – made worse by accumulation – by indicating that students qualifying for various indices of deprivation entering university are somehow disadvantaged by their prior entry qualification, prior attainment in school, or continued underperformance at the university which subsequently lands them in lower level jobs. Social capital seems to play a crucial role in determining trajectories. We argue that most of these problems are inter-related. Students qualifying for various deprivation indicators are similar in several aspects and often go on to have similar trajectories. They are very likely to underachieve in GCSEs, take up inferior qualifications, dropout or complete courses with a grade which cannot be cashed in very well in the labour market. This makes the entire issue of intergenerational mobility very complex.

More recently, the relatively unexplored and slightly controversial arena of socio-genomics has tried to link social mobility and achievement to genes and heritability. Thompson (2014), for example, shows the correlation between income and education varies greatly across groups of children with different versions of a specific gene called monoamine-oxidase A (MAOA). This gene impacts neurotransmission activity, exists in two genetically variant forms, and both forms are equally distributed in the human population. Children with one of these genetic variants showed a positive association between household income and education. However, this relationship was much weaker in children with the other variant of the gene, who comprise over half of the population.

These results were still valid when the interactive effects were identified and studied using genetic variation between full biological siblings. This finding is crucial because genetic principles asserted via biological siblings is as good as being randomly assigned or being a random sample for investigation.

Direct measurement of human genotypes is now a reasonably straightforward process. Another similar study conducted by Turkheimer, Haley, Waldron, d'Onofrio, and Gottesman (2003), showed the heritability of IQ is greater among high SES families than it is among lower SES families. One of the explanations given was that interactive complementarities exist between genetic and environmental advantages and together these influence cognitive skills. An important methodological distinction can be made between studies that regress child outcomes onto parent outcomes and studies that use genetic markers to study heritability and intergenerational mobility. A good example of the latter can be studies which sample different types of twins or adoptees to decompose the proportion of variation in a characteristic that is attributable to genetic versus environmental influences. The decomposition approach has tended to find a larger overall role for genetic factors, while the regression approach is more amenable to incorporating genetic data to estimate gene-environment interactions. While behavioural genetics and studies building on social science continue to challenge each other for methodological rigour they continue to hint at similar findings – students from disadvantaged backgrounds are likely to take up non-traditional routes, have lower attainment, and poorer labour market outcomes compared to their peers.

The strength of longitudinal data sets available in the UK are now recognised globally. These resources have given the UK social science community a competitive advantage in understanding critical population trajectories over the life course and across changing contexts. By building on the rapidly expanding access to greater quantities of administrative data, and drawing expertise form various fields and via novel advances as the ones mentioned in this chapter there is considerable opportunity to implement innovative approaches by tracking key social groups in a period of rapid change. For example, it is now possible to track younger cohorts of students qualifying for various deprivation indicators follow them up across the student life-cycle to answer crucial policy and research questions.

Who Takes Up a Vocational Route?

Free and compulsory education is provided to all students by the state until the age of 16. At the end of year 11 in secondary schools, most 16-year-olds take GCSEs in a range of core and optional subjects. After taking GCSE examinations, a majority of students continue with further academic qualifications while some prefer a slightly different experience. They explore options other than classroom-based teaching in sixth form and further education colleges via a vocational route. These students may choose to seek employment, training or a vocational qualification. An even smaller proportion of students take a gap year or drop out of education. Young people who are not in education, employment or training (NEET) are often those who are from a disadvantaged background.

Literature shows the formation of educational preferences is predisposed by cultural capital (Winkle-Wagner, 2010). Such notions are often inherent in the family in active or dormant state and continue to influence school success. For example, students with higher attainment often prefer the university sector while those who have not been doing so well in school often steer into the non-university sector. To add to this, the highly selective education system in the UK means that those from certain social class have more support, options and are continued to be looked at favourably by selective elite institutions held in high esteem. This can have a long-standing influence on students continuing into the labour market. Contrary to policy claims, vocational orientation is only weakly connected to preferences, whereas high-status orientation is the main factor determining the choice of university sector (Ahola & Nurmi, 2006).

This argument is supported by statistics released by the DfE for the academic year 2017–2018. Making use of student destination data, the analysis shows after completing key stage four (finishing year 11, usually aged 16) 94% of pupils were in education, employment or apprenticeships, with 86% staying in an education setting. After completing key stage five (taking A-levels or other level three qualifications, usually aged 18) 89% of students stayed in education, employment and apprenticeships over the period, with 61% staying in education. Thus, more students drop out of education at the end of key stage five, aged 18.

The data also shows that a significantly lower proportion of disadvantaged students participate in 16–18 study than other students. DfE reports young people as having sustained destination if they attend and spend the first two terms of the academic year (five of the six months during their destination year, October–March) at one or more education provider, in employment or in a combination of the two. When the time spent is considered only in the context of education this is referred to as the sustained education destination. Among students who were at the end of key stage four in state-funded schools in 2015/2016, 88% of disadvantaged pupils were recorded in a sustained destination, with 80% in a sustained education destination, compared with 96% of all other pupils in a sustained destination and 89% in a sustained education destination. Thus a majority of those who leave school at the age of 16 are from working class origins. The division of school and examination systems are also replicated by a division between those who attend school sixth forms, sixth form colleges and further education colleges. Some research suggests that, even within the same school in the same building, experiences of working class children differ (Guardian, 2017). Thus, students qualifying for deprivation indicators are slightly more likely to drop out of education or enter an employment destination (4%) after key stage 4 compared to all other pupils (3%).

Non-disadvantaged students are more likely to enter level 3 study during the age of 16–18 years than disadvantaged students. In 2018, 15.5% of A-level, 23.2% of applied general and 23.3% of technical level students in state-funded schools and colleges were from a disadvantaged background. Thus, relatively higher proportion of students who entered applied general and technical level qualifications were disadvantaged, compared to students who entered A-levels. Just as shown for level 3, disadvantaged students were also over-represented in level 2 vocational qualifications. In 2018, 33.3% of level 2 vocational students and 32.2% of technical certificate students in state-funded institutions were reported as disadvantaged at the end of key stage 4, compared to 27.7% in the potential cohort. This pattern is similar to that of the previous year 2017. Thus, students who take up vocational qualifications are more likely to come from a disadvantaged background, lack cultural capital and are seen less favourably by admissions decision-makers in the higher education sector. Put together, these heavily impact their life chances and social mobility, often locking them in intergenerational poverty.

Vocational Qualifications: By Choice, Force or Providence

One of the several possible reasons for students picking up different qualification routes is linked to their differential prior attainment. While career guidance and advisory services available in secondary schools benefit many students, narratives of prior experiences from students – particularly of those from a disadvantaged background with lower attainment – often highlight how they were encouraged by the school to take up a vocational route as their teachers did not think they could perform well in the academic route. In the absence of a direct comparator, it is difficult to guess whether these students could have done better had they been allowed to take up qualifications with a more academic focus.

Statistical modelling enables us to predict attainment with remarkable accuracy by making use of individual-level measures such as social class as there is a strong correlation between these variables. Working class students are known to do less well academically than their middle-class peers. A number of reasons have been cited to explain this differential achievement including poverty, family expectations, assumptions about ability, cultural capital, parental involvement in schooling, cultures and practices of educational institutions themselves (Banerjee, 2016). Working class students do not just do less well in examinations; we also find a higher proportion of these students in non-traditional educational routes and qualifications. Those routes which are more likely to be taken by working class pupils are widely considered to be of a lower status and are less likely to lead to admissions to elite universities when compared to their middle-class peers. The academic/vocational divide finds its base in these choices.

Wage premiums or the typical salaries earned by students who pursue academic qualifications are generally higher than for students from vocational qualifications. However, academic routes take a relatively longer time period to complete (Dearden, McIntosh, Myck, & Vignoles, 2002). Not only can vocational qualifications be completed in a shorter period of time, but they are also seen as a preparation for the world of work – which may appeal to some students, and disadvantaged students in particular, who may be wanting to start working quickly to manage their depleting resources and deal with financial hardships. As the teaching and training are based on scenarios linked to the workplace, vocational route students may find a job sooner than those following academic routes, albeit these may be lower level jobs and may offer a lower pay. Depending on whether it is the long-term goal or immediate need, student finance and labour market outcomes could be equally important factors among others which motivate students to choose between available qualification routes.

Learning and training in vocational education emphasises the acquisition of technical skills and knowledge. Right from the start, it nurtures behavioural competence in VEQ students which is required at work. This is one of the most beneficial aspects of the vocational route. However, often what is overlooked and is equally crucial is the relationship between learning and the learner's identity. Learning is defined as a process of *becoming* and invariably learning cultures transform those who enter them. Learner-specific characteristics such as gender, family background, social class and so on influence this experience but may not be sufficient for effective learning and training or relevant qualification can play a significant role in providing a head start.

Although the contributions made by taught behavioural competence may be crucial, the other important element which cannot be ignored is the habitus. Vocational habitus refers to the occupational choices an individual makes. It describes who they are, based on the upbringing, the people and situations which may have influenced them in several ways while they were growing up. Vocational habitus can thus explain central aspect of students' experiences during the student life-cycle. There can be an idealised and a realised self, depending on how they oriented to a particular set of dispositions (Colley, James, Diment, & Tedder, 2007). Vocational habitus may be helpful in reinforcing and developing these according to demands at the workplace; however, it may very well also be responsible for reproducing social inequalities. In the academic literature available, while the impact of vocational habitus on work and occupational choices has been highlighted, whether this equally impacts young people's decisions of taking vocational routes remains unclear. However, if it does, it is clearly a barrier impeding social mobility (Colley et al., 2007).

Undergraduate Admission Patterns by Prior Qualification

Entry to higher education in the UK is largely determined by prior educational achievement, as entrants are expected to possess the necessary qualifications at an appropriate level. In England, the school to HE transition is mediated by the Universities and Colleges Admissions Service (UCAS). The application and admissions process to undergraduate courses involves various stages and a series of choices made by applicants as well as admissions decision-makers. The outcome is determined not just by examination results but also by university policies and decisions made by selectors. In the absence of a centralised admissions procedure, higher education institutions (HEIs) enjoy the autonomy to decide which candidate is a 'good fit' for the course.

Selective admissions are one of the most debated outcomes of HE expansion: universities have the power to influence their student populations through determining which students may enter their institution. Recruitment mechanisms adopted by universities can also play a significant role in shaping the applicant pool. This may happen unintentionally when institutions appear more or less attractive to particular students (Barham, 2011). In the absence of an obligation to accept any applicant who completes school-leaving qualifications, universities directly select students from among the applicant pool, exercising discretion to choose between available applicants (West & Barham, 2009). When a selective university admits an applicant, it could be because they are creating a class, or perhaps choosing students who are more likely to succeed at the university or are the best available in the pool.

The socio-economic mix of students attending various universities is a significant form of status differentiation between UK universities (Crawford & Greaves, 2015; Crawford et al., 2016). This is not explicitly mentioned in university mission group statements or policy documents but essentially contributes to different estimations of university prestige (Boliver, 2015; Croxford & Raffe, 2014; Raffe & Croxford, 2013). For example, students from more advantaged social-class backgrounds and private schools are especially over-represented at the universities of Oxford, Cambridge and the rest of the Russell Group, whereas students from 'non-traditional backgrounds' are concentrated in new, post-1992 universities with widening access remits (Boliver, 2011, 2013, 2015; Hemsley-Brown, 2015).

Substantial differences are also noted in HE participation rates generally and at high-status universities more specifically by socio-economic background (Chowdry, Crawford, Dearden, Goodman, & Vignoles, 2013). The differences are substantially reduced once the prior achievement is included. These findings hold for both state and private school pupils. Chowdry et al. (2013) conclude that poor performance in secondary schools is more important in explaining lower HE participation rates among pupils from lower SES than barriers arising at the point of entry to HE.

There are substantial differences in university entry overall and at Russell Group institutions between students from high- and low-income families. However, most of this difference is driven by application decisions, particularly once 'ability' at age 11 is controlled (Anders, 2012, LSYPE). The income gradients in university participation are not necessarily driven by discrimination against students from lower income backgrounds. Instead, poorer students are less likely to apply. Policies intending to provide equal opportunities by reducing the university participation gap at the point of entry are likely to face small rewards compared to those which ensure students from poorer backgrounds have the necessary qualifications to apply.

In the context of prior qualifications, the vocational route has also been a matter of much debate (Ertl, Hayward, & McLaughlin, 2012), particularly the transition from vocational to Higher Education. Admission staff note meritocracy should continue to be the gold standard for fairness in admissions. Investigations into how applications from students with vocational qualifications are perceived and processed show these are done with the aim to enable institutions to meet institutional priorities and are not necessarily meant to offer equal opportunities (Leathwood & Hutchings, 2003). It should not come as a surprise then that VEQ students are relatively under-represented at elite universities and in courses held in high esteem.

Which University?

Prospective students complete an application via the UCAS. The information provided also includes UCAS tariff points. These are scores allocated to applicants on the same scale to enable comparisons of different qualifications. Selective universities which are held in high esteem such as those in the Russell Group accept students with relatively higher tariff scores and are termed as high tariff providers. Similarly, there are middle and lower tariff providers. The data shows BTEC students were less likely to study at a Russell Group university and were relatively more likely to study at low-tariff providers (Figure 1).

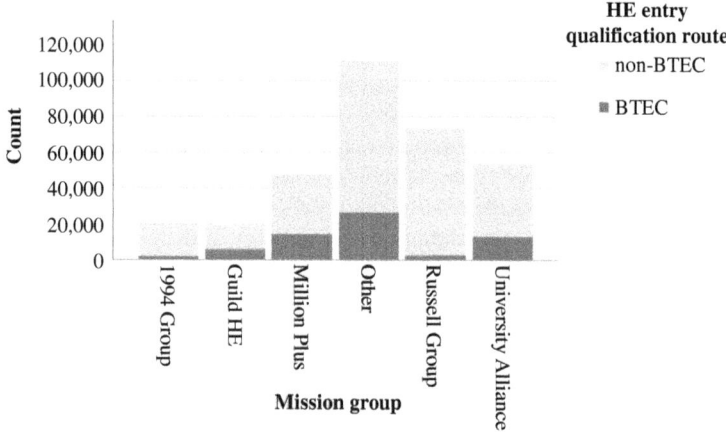

Figure 1. Undergraduate Students in Higher Education by Qualification Route and Provider.

Undergraduate Subject Areas

The Joint Academic Coding System (JACS) is a way of classifying academic subjects and modules in higher education. The system is co-owned and maintained by HESA and UCAS. The summary statistics presented in Figure 2 follows this classification. According to this classification, there are 19 major subject areas in higher education. Compared to other subject areas, a relatively higher proportion of vocational route students were studying subjects like Creative Arts and Design, Business and Administrative Studies, Biological

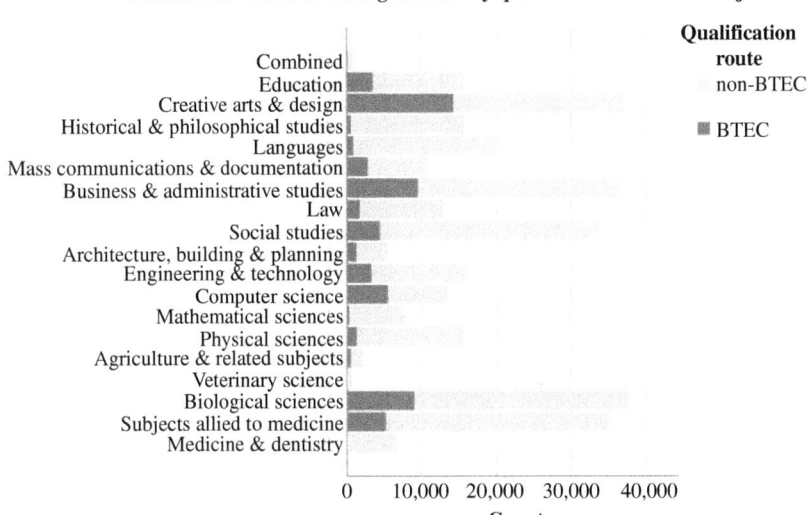

Figure 2. Students with BTEC Qualifications in Undergraduate Courses.

Sciences, subjects allied to Medicine, Computer Science and Social Studies. It could be that these were some of the more popular subject choices among BTEC students for the undergraduate course. Another possibility could be that BTEC students were more likely to be accepted in these courses – either due to their skill set or curriculum. Though the higher education landscape is beginning to change, all providers do not offer admissions to students from a vocational route such as BTEC. Similarly, BTEC students are not necessarily accepted into all courses, for example, courses with high returns such as STEM. Figure 2 shows the proportion of students by prior qualification in undergraduate courses across various subject areas.

These findings were also supported by the statistical analysis of admissions data from universities who were collaborating for the Transforming Transitions project. Three main subject areas were considered for the analysis as these were being offered across all partner universities. The analysis showed overall BTEC students were more likely to be offered a place in Sports and Exercise Science and least likely to study Computer Science (Banerjee, 2018a, 2018b, 2018c; Banerjee & Myhill, 2019).

The HEPI report (2019), 'Reaching the parts of society universities have missed: A manifesto for the new Director for Fair Access and Participation', summarises a collection of action points for the new Office for Students on unlocking access to higher education. There are several under-represented groups in HE as some social groups are known to shy away from the university. Then there are other students who take up qualifications which prioritise learning-by-doing, for example, the BTECs, as their curriculum is linked to work-based scenarios. Yet a growing number of students taking up these courses in further education colleges are now moving on to higher education. It is, therefore, more important than ever before to investigate the experiences and outcomes of these overlooked group of students, who move from vocational to higher education.

Degree Outcomes

We analysed progression data for the Transforming Transitions project by qualification routes for the subject areas of Business, Computer Science, Sports and Exercise Science. The analysis showed the highest proportion of those who failed their end of first-year examination were vocational route entrants and had a BTEC only qualification (Banerjee, 2018a, 2018b, 2018c; Banerjee & Myhill, 2019). However, although the progression for BTEC students from the first to the second year of study is lower than traditional entry students, the vast majority of BTEC students do succeed and are particularly more successful in Sports and Exercise Science. The other important finding from the analysis was that most BTEC students qualified for one or more set of criteria used to flag deprivation indices. Thus, it is very likely that, in addition to prior qualifications, there are other factors involved which impact progression of BTEC students.

One of the degree outcome measures used by HESA is the classification of a first degree and it indicates the qualification class obtained upon completion of the course. In the analysis reported here there were six different categories: *first, second (upper and lower), third, unclassified* and *not applicable*. Certain qualifications obtained at first degree level are not subject to classification of award, notably medical and general degrees. These, together with aegrotat qualifications (where a certificate has been provided stating that a university student is too ill to attend an examination) are included within the *Unclassified* category. Third-class honours, fourth-class honours and pass have been aggregated as Third/pass. Lower second and undivided second-class honours have been aggregated as Lower second.

Figure 3 shows most students – from BTEC routes or otherwise – qualified with an upper-second-class honours. However, the next highest subcategory of degree outcome classification for BTEC students was a lower second showing fewer vocational entry qualification route students do go on to achieve a 2:1. The next category with more students from academic routes was a first-class honours. There were no BTEC students in the unclassified category in Figure 3 which supports the findings represented in Figure 2 that medicine and dentistry degrees do not have BTEC entrants.

Patterns of Progression

HESA administers surveys to students when they have completed the course in order to capture the trajectories pursued by those who qualify from UK Universities. The target population of the Destination of Leavers in Higher

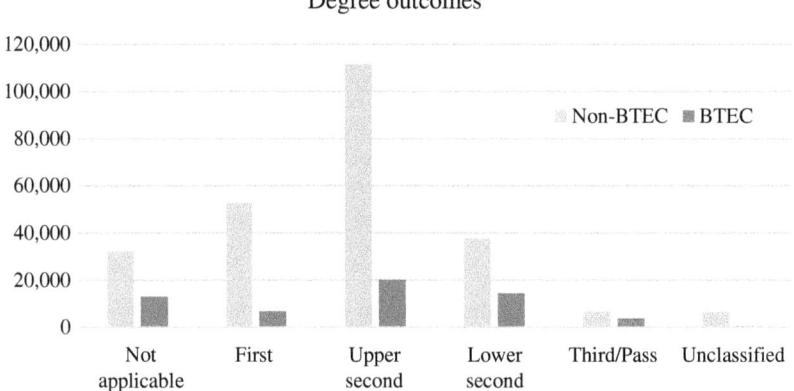

Figure 3. Degree Outcomes by HE Entry Prior Qualification Route.

Education (DLHE) survey includes all students reported to HESA for the reporting period 01 August to 31 July as obtaining relevant higher education qualifications. All students are included, irrespective of whether they had pursued the course full-time or part-time. Sandwich students and those writing up theses are also included in these surveys. Postgraduate research students who receive awards from dormant status are also included in the target population. The analysis presented in this chapter mapped activity of UK domiciled students who had enroled at an English university to study for a first degree and were registered as full-time students. These students were from the cohort who had entered university in 2012/2013 and had graduated by 2016–2017 from a three- or four-year undergraduate course.

As the data set is quite rich, it contains a lot of information and has different categories of students. The first step in the analysis was to exclude certain 'outlier' categories. For example, some students do not necessarily complete an undergraduate course and leave with further education level qualifications. Some students are registered at a UK university for their course but end up spending a significant amount of time studying overseas. Universities also have incoming exchange students for example who are on an intercalated course so while they are registered elsewhere at their primary university, they spend time in the UK studying for their course. The data also has a record of any deceased student during this period. All these categories were excluded from the target population. While universities encourage leavers to complete the DLHE survey, ineligibility or explicit refusals are not uncommon. Such students were also excluded from the population for destination data.

The way this survey is designed to capture data differentiates between full-time and part-time work. Being in full-time work denotes these leavers consider their most important activity to be working full-time. Other activities pursued by these students did not include further study either full-time or part-time and they were not undertaking training or research. However, if there are some students who are due to start a job in the next month and whose activities include working full-time, they are included in this category. After graduating from university, more students who had non-BTEC qualifications were in full-time employment. Similarly, part-time work included those who indicated their most important activity was working part-time, and whose other activities did not include either full-time or part-time further study, training or research. It also includes those where the most important activity was due to start a job in the next month and other activities included working part-time but not working full-time. Relatively more BTEC students were working part-time compared to other students.

The preceding category captures students who are only working and have not taken up any additional activity. There are two more categories which identify students who may have taken up more than one activity, for example, they may be studying and working simultaneously and one of them could be a full-time engagement. Students identifying with the category *primarily in work and also studying*, as the name suggests, includes those who indicated their most important activity was working full-time or part-time, and whose other activities included full-time or part-time study, training or research. There was another similar category named *primarily studying and also in work* and included those who indicated their most important activity was full-time or part-time study, training or research, and whose other activities included working full-time or part-time. There were fewer BTEC students in both categories compared to non-BTEC students.

Leavers who were studying or were in training or research were classified separately. *Full-time study* included those leavers who indicated their most important activity was full-time further study, training or research, and whose other activities did not include working full-time or part-time. It also includes those where the most important activity was due to start a job in the next month, and an additional activity included full-time further study, training or research, provided that working full-time was not also reported as an activity. *Part-time study* includes those who indicated their most important activity was part-time further study, training or research, and whose other activities did not include working full-time or part-time. Due to start work includes those who indicated in their most important activity that they were due to start a job in the next month, but neither working full-time, working part-time, or further study was reported as an activity. There were fewer BTEC students in all three categories explained before.

Unemployed leavers were the ones who indicated so in the DLHE survey. Marginally higher BTEC students were unemployed. The *Other* category includes those whose most important activity was either taking time out in order to travel or doing something else. There were slightly more non-BTEC students in this last category. These results have been summarised in Figure 4. For most categories, there were marginal differences between BTEC and non-BTEC students and the major difference was in the *not applicable* category. When a student is put in this category it means no record of employment activity has

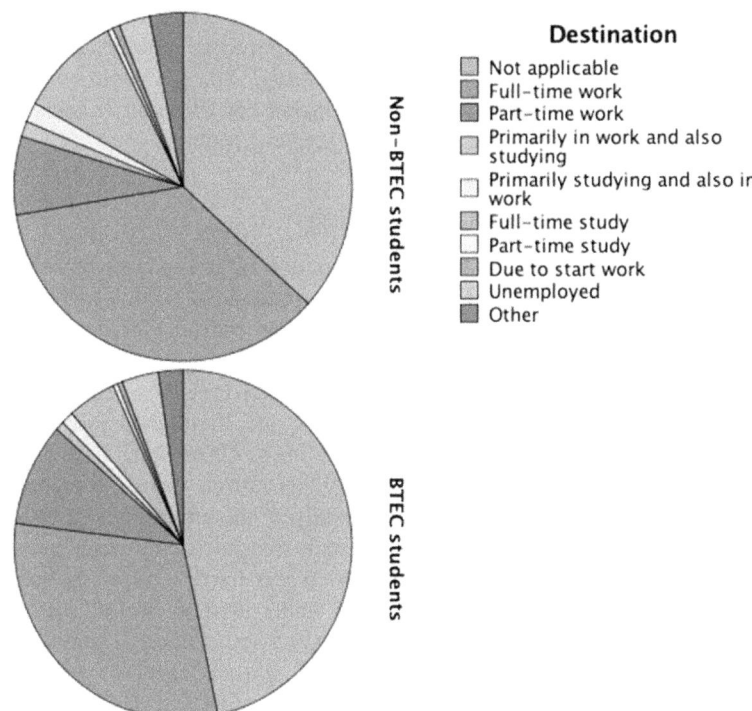

Figure 4. Destination of Leavers in Higher Education: BTEC versus Non-BTEC Students.

been found. So we do not know whether these students are in employment, training, studying or unemployed. More BTEC students were in this category.

VEQ students are not always accepted on to STEM courses or by elite universities, yet a growing number of students with vocational qualifications, such as the BTECs, are now taking up undergraduate courses. In 2016, one in four students entering HE held a BTEC qualification, double the 2008 figure (Gicheva & Petrie, 2018). It is therefore more important than even before to understand how these students perform at the university transitioning from their vocational entry route to a more academically focussed, HE degree. Research conducted by the Higher Education Funding Council of England (HEFCE, now Office for Students) has supported these claims by showing that the biggest factor driving variations in student outcomes nationally is the entry qualification of students. For example, BTEC students have a smaller proportion of "good" degrees than all students with A-levels – even BTEC students with three distinctions get a smaller proportion than A-level students with three Cs (HEFCE, 2018).

This reiterates the questions raised earlier concerning whether the BTEC route is working for progression to higher education (Huntley, 2018). BTEC students are now being looked as the widening participation cohort who have been overlooked in the past. As BTEC qualifications are now being acknowledged as contributing to widening HE access (Kelly, 2017), it might be the case that a more collaborative approach between higher education providers and FE colleges can support the progression of these students better.

Parity between Different Qualifications

Universities with the highest widening participation rates also have higher dropout rates. It may be that students from different qualification routes have different skill sets and not all of these are suited for pursuing higher academic qualifications. Evidence for this comes from the fact that an increasing number of students from vocational routes are now entering HE (UCAS, 2019). Despite being motivated to pursue a higher education degree, the highest proportion of those who fail their end of first-year examinations at Universities have a BTEC prior qualification (Banerjee & Myhill, 2019). However, degree outcomes are not predestined and often the first year of study at the university can be transformational, especially for entrants from disadvantaged backgrounds and non-traditional qualification routes. One of the biggest barriers faced by students from non-traditional routes is their limited understanding of HE assessment practices which is very different from further education colleges. The differences in course work and academic skills may add further layers of complexity. A-level students, for example, may have stronger maths and academic writing skills whereas BTEC students may have stronger presentation skills (see chapter 6), highlighting how curriculum can help students to develop transferable skills.

The Social Mobility Commission report (2019) says at 16 disadvantaged students are more likely to enter further education than school sixth forms but the FE sector is overlooked and needs funds to give students high-quality education. The National Strategy for Access and Student Success in Higher Education (2014), developed by the Department for Business for Innovation and Skills' (BIS), discusses vocational qualifications in relation to access. It is now becoming increasingly important to include students with vocational qualifications in the demographic groups for which BIS monitors retention and success. This is because vocational route students do struggle to pass their end of first-year examination which is often the biggest hurdle for them. However, once they go past this, most of them go on to complete their degrees and a majority of them do obtain an upper second class with honours in their first degrees (Banerjee & Myhill, 2019). The OfS could lead the change by including students with vocational qualifications in their monitoring and reporting (Shields & Masardo, 2015) towards addressing barriers to student success.

Conclusion

Students from disadvantaged backgrounds are more likely to drop out of education compared to their middle-class peers at the end of key stage 4 and key stage 5. These dropout rates are higher at the end of key stage 5. Significantly lower proportion of disadvantaged students participate in 16–18 studies than other students. Disadvantaged pupils are slightly more likely to enter an employment destination (4%) after key stage 4 compared to all other pupils (3%). Further, disadvantaged students are over-represented in level 3 and level 2 vocational qualifications. This choice is linked to differential achievement which can be explained by poverty, family expectations, assumptions about ability, cultural capital, parental involvement in schooling, cultures and practices of educational institutions themselves. BTEC students are less likely to study at high tariff providers which are selective in admitting students and according to the just-released UCAS admission cycle report, the numbers have fallen (UCAS, 2019). Working class students are more likely to choose vocational routes and these routes are not necessarily accepted by universities as entry routes to undergraduate courses. Thus, a majority of students leave with further education qualifications. Statistical analysis shows most students who had followed a vocational route to HE were enroled in undergraduate courses at low-tariff providers. They were more likely to study creative arts and least likely to study medicine. BTEC students reportedly struggle during the first year of study due to limitations in academic skills. The highest proportion of those who fail their end of first-year examination are the ones who had only BTEC qualifications. Progression patterns show degree outcomes are not necessarily predetermined and a majority of BTEC students do pass with an upper second and secure employment.

There are two main points to note here. First, a majority of vocational entry qualification students are from a disadvantaged background. However, they do not necessarily lack academic potential. The first year of higher education can be transformational (Banerjee & Myhill, 2019) as can be support offered during the age of 14–19 years. For this quite often overlooked widening participation cohort, their success or failure is closely aligned to their limited understanding of knowing the ropes or having the opportunities than lacking the motivation to succeed or achieve.

References

Ahola, S., & Nurmi, J. (2006). *Choosing university or vocational college: The formation of educational preferences* (pp. 127–139). Retrieved from https://doi.org/10.1080/0031383970410202

Anders, J. (2012). The link between household income, university applications and university attendance. *Fiscal Studies, 33*(2), 185–210.

Banerjee, P. A. (2016). A systematic review of factors linked to poor academic performance of disadvantaged students in science and maths in schools. *Cogent Education, 3*(1). doi:10.1080/2331186X.2016.1178441

Banerjee, P. A. (2018a). Widening participation in higher education with a view to implementing institutional change. *Perspectives: Policy and Practice in Higher Education, 22*(3), 75–81. doi:10.1080/13603108.2018.1441198

Banerjee, P. A. (2018b). How successful are BTEC students at the University? *Wonkhe.* Retrieved from https://wonkhe.com/blogs/how-successful-are-btec-students-at-university/

Banerjee, P. A. (2018c). How likely are BTEC students to enter higher education? *Society for research in higher education.* Retrieved from https://srheblog.com/2018/04/24/how-likely-are-btec-students-to-enter-higher-education/

Banerjee, P. A., & Myhill, D. (under review 2019). Does prior qualification affect degree outcomes? *Journal of Further and Higher Education.*

Barham, E. (2011). *Markets, selection and equity: How reputation and popularity influence student admissions and recruitment in universities in England.* London: London School of Economics and Political Science (LSE). Retrieved from http://etheses.lse.ac.uk/3119/

BIS. (2014). Report by the Department for Business for Innovation and Skills. National Strategy for Access and Student Success in Higher Education. Retrieved from www.gov.uk

Boliver, V. (2011). Expansion, differentiation, and the persistence of social class inequalities in British higher education. *Higher Education, 61*(3), 229–242.

Boliver, V. (2013). How fair is access to more prestigious UK universities? *The British Journal of Sociology, 64*(2), 344–364. doi:10.1111/1468-4446.12021

Boliver, V. (2015). Are there distinctive clusters of higher and lower status universities in the UK? *Oxford Review of Education, 41*(5), 608–627. doi:10.1080/03054985.2015.1082905

Chowdry, H., Crawford, C., Dearden, L., Goodman, A., & Vignoles, A. (2013). Widening participation in higher education: analysis using linked administrative data: *Widening Participation in Higher Education. Journal of the Royal Statistical Society: Series A (Statistics in Society), 176*(2), 431–457. doi:10.1111/j.1467-985X.2012.01043.x

Colley, H., James, D., Diment, K., & Tedder, M. (2007). *Learning as becoming in vocational education and training: Class, gender and the role of vocational habitus* (pp. 471–498). Retrieved from https://doi.org/10.1080/13636820300200240

Crawford, C. (2014). *Socio-economic differences in university outcomes in the UK: drop-out, degree completion and degree class.* IFS Working Papers. Retrieved from https://www.econstor.eu/handle/10419/119553

Crawford, C., & Greaves, E. (2015). Socio-economic, ethnic and gender differences in HE participation. Department of Business, Innovation and Skills. 1 BIS RESEARCH PAPER NO. 186.

Crawford, C., Gregg, P., Macmillan, L., Vignoles, A., & Wyness, G. (2016). Higher education, career opportunities, and intergenerational inequality. *Oxford Review of Economic Policy, 32*(4), 553–575.

Croxford, L., & Raffe, D. (2014). Social class, ethnicity and access to higher education in the four countries of the UK: 1996–2010. *International Journal of Lifelong Education, 33*(1), 77–95.

Dearden, L., McIntosh, S., Myck, M., & Vignoles, A. (2002). The returns to academic and vocational qualifications in Britain. Retrieved from https://doi.org/10.1111/1467-8586.00152

Ertl, H., Hayward, G., & McLaughlin, J. (2012). The transition from vocational to higher education from the perspective of higher education admission staff. In *The future of vocational education and training in a changing world* (pp. 63−82). Wiesbaden, Germany: Verlag für Sozialwissenschaften.

Gicheva, N., & Petrie, K. (2018). V*ocation, vocation, vocation: the role of vocational routes into higher education*. Social Market Foundation Report. Retrieved from www.smf.co.uk

Gill, T., (2017). Preparing students for university study: A statistical comparison of different post-16 qualifications. *Research Papers in Education, 33*(3), 1−19.

Gill, T., & Vidal Rodeiro, C. L. (2014). *Predictive validity of level 3 qualifications: Extended Project, Cambridge Pre-U, International Baccalaureate, BTEC Diploma*. Cambridge Assessment Research Report. Cambridge: Cambridge Assessment.

Green, F., & Vignoles, A., (2012). An empirical method for deriving grade equivalence for university entrance qualifications: An application to A-levels and the International Baccalaureate. *Oxford Review of Education, 38*(4), 473−491.

Greenback, P. (2009). *Widening participation and social class*. Retrieved from https://www.researchgate.net/publication/273768422_Widening_participation_and_social_class. Accessed on April 4, 2017.

HEFCE. (2018). *Differences in student outcomes: The effect of student characteristics*. Report available from HEFCE archives. Retrieved from www.hefce.ac.uk

Hemsley-Brown, J. (2015). Getting into a Russell group university: High scores and private schooling. *British Educational Research Journal, 41*(3), 398−422.

Huntley, G. (2018). Universities must revisit BTECs as a route to higher education. *Wonkhe*. London.

Kelly, S. (2017). Reforming BTECs: Applied general qualifications as a route to higher education. HEPI report. Retrieved from www.hepi.ac.uk

Leathwood, C., & Hutchings, M. (2003). *Entry routes to higher education. Higher education and social class: Issues of exclusion and inclusion*. In Archer, L., Hutchings, M., & Ross, A. London: Routledge Farmer.

McCoy, T., & Adamson, D. (2016). Building a House on Sand? In Steventon, G., Cureton, D., & Clouder, L. (Eds.). *Student Attainment in Higher Education: Issues, Controversies and Debates*. Abingdon: Routledge. 161−173.

Raffe, D., & Croxford, L. (2013). One system or four? Cross-border applications and entries to full-time undergraduate courses in the UK since devolution: One system or four? *Higher Education Quarterly, 67*(2), 111−134. doi:10.1111/hequ.12009

Reay, D., Crozier, G., & Clayton, J. (2009). 'Fitting in' or 'standing out': Working-class students in UK higher education. *British Educational Research Journal, 36*(1), 107−124.

Rouncefield-Swales, A. (2014). *Vocational progression to selecting universities comparisons and trends 2010−2013*. Retrieved from http://www.careerpilot.org.uk/upload/Final_BTEC_Research_2014.pdf. Accessed on April 4, 2017.

Shields, R., & Masardo, A. (2015). *Changing patterns in vocational entry qualifications, student support and outcomes in undergraduate degree programmes*. Higher Education Academy. Retrieved from www.heacademy.ac.uk

Social Mobility Commission (SMC). (2016). *State of the nation 2016: Social mobility in Great Britain*. Retrieved from www.gov.uk

Social Mobility Commission (SMC). (2019). *Social mobility in Great Britain − State of the nation 2018 to 2019. SMC report: Research and analysis*. Social Mobility Commission. Retrieved from www.gov.uk

The Guardian. (2017). *Working-class children get less of everything in education – Including respect*. Retrieved from https://www.theguardian.com

The HEPI report. (2019). Reaching the parts of society universities have missed: A manifesto for the new director for fair access and participation. Higher education policy institute. Available to download here www.hepi.ac.uk

Thompson, O. (2014, Spring) Economic background and educational attainment: The role of gene-environment interactions. *Journal of Human Resources*, University of Wisconsin Press, *49*(2), 263–294. doi:10.1353/jhr.2014.0012

Turkheimer, E., Haley, A., Waldron, M., d'Onofrio, B., & Gottesman, I. I. (2003). Socioeconomic status modifies heritability of IQ in young children. *Psychological Science*, *14*(6), 623–628.

UCAS. (2019). *UCAS undergraduate end of cycle report*. Retrieved from www.ucas.com

West, A., & Barham, E. (2009). Student mobility, qualifications and academic recognition in the EU. *Assessment in Education: Principles, Policy & Practice*, *16*(1): 25–37.

Winkle-Wagner, R. (2010). Cultural capital: The promises and pitffalls in education research. AEHE, *36*(1), 1–144.

Chapter 4

Ways of Learning: Student Voices on Learning Experiences across the Transition

Debra Myhill and Sara Venner

Introduction

In this chapter, and the two which follow, we share the voiced experiences of students to inform our understanding of the transition from school or Further Education (FE) college into university. The data which underpin this draw on a series of 39 interviews or focus groups with 64 students in both FE and HE. The FE students were all second-year vocational students at the end of their courses, whereas the HE students were all in their first year at university. Three groups formed the HE sample: students with a vocational entry qualification only; students with a vocational qualification and an A-level entry qualification; and students with an A-level or IB entry qualification. Having these three groups allowed us to compare across the entry routes and to avoid making unevidenced assumptions about one group. For consistency, we will refer to these three groups as vocational students, A-level students, and vocational plus A-level students throughout this book.

In contrast to the statistical data about entry qualifications and progression, the interview data allowed us to understand the diversity and differences of these students' experience of transition from their own perspectives, and to compare whether these differences linked to their qualification route into university. What the interviews also revealed was some of the ways in which their transition experience had highlighted barriers or challenges which might explain some of the differential outcomes in progression and attainment.

This chapter focuses specifically on learning experiences, and ways of learning, considering how academically well-prepared the students felt for their chosen university courses, and how similar or different they found the ways of learning at university compared with their pre-university learning. The chapter addresses both the transition challenges experienced by students in terms of subject knowledge and skills, and their experiences and preferences in terms of ways of learning.

Academic Literacy

Although the term 'academic literacy' is in widespread use, there is quite considerable variety in what it means, from referring simply to the kind of writing required at university, to including all elements of communication, and numerical literacy. Perhaps the most common way to understand academic literacy is 'proficiency in reading and writing about academic subjects, with the goal of contributing to the ongoing conversations of an academic field' (Neeley, 2005, p. 8). Certainly, the comments from the students were most likely to refer to the demands of reading and writing at university. Academic literacy is important in terms of progression and achievement at universities because achievement remains predominantly assessed through students' written work, and particularly the written essay.

A majority of the first-year university students, irrespective of qualification upon entry, commented that different aspects of academic literacy had presented challenges for them. The reading and understanding of academic texts, particularly academic journals, was one problematic area. Comments indicated that students did not feel prepared because engaging with this new style of reading was unfamiliar. This view is illustrated by an A-level student who reflected that 'I'd never encountered journals before really, or if I had, I'd only sort of stumbled on it accidentally. [Laughs] Um, so yeah that's quite alien'. Furthermore, difficulties were encountered due to the structure of academic articles. As one A-level student said, this change was 'daunting' to adjust to, making the understanding of text troublesome:

> Maybe just reading academic texts, the articles. I'm not used to the article format, like seeing the abstract and the method and the discussion and whatever it is. Yeah, I'm not really used to that so I found that quite daunting. So, because when you want to write a good essay you want to include as much academic text as possible, but if you don't understand them I think it's quite hard to use them in your essay.

A few students also found reading academic text hard because of the frequent use of new subject-specific abbreviations, and subject-specific vocabulary, as highlighted by a vocational student: 'I think with the reading as well, it takes longer because I feel like every few sentences I'm looking up like a word because I didn't know what it meant'.

Some of the challenges related to academic reading concerned surprise at the expectations of wider reading on their courses. Wider reading demands some independence as a learner, as one vocational student explained:

> I think I especially have found the fact that they leave you to your own devices a lot, they kind of just go 'Right this is it'. And then they expect you to find everything yourself – because we should be able to do that, but that's something I've had to get

used to doing. Like they kind of expect you to read around everything, even though when we first came we didn't know we had to do that.

Some students highlighted specific difficulties when locating and searching for credible peer-reviewed sources:

> I've come up with this strategy – I Google and then it takes me to Wikipedia and then, you know how Wikipedia it does referencing also, so I look at the sources where it came and then I go all the way back to them and I reference them. So, it makes it much easier. But the first time I saw it, I was like, how am I supposed to find a peer reviewed essay on you know, this and that? It was really, really hard, definitely hard.

Adjusting to the volume of reading required during the first year of study prompted a few students to say that they would have liked more guidance about which specific key texts they should read, particularly at the beginning of the academic year. To highlight the problems faced, one vocational plus A-level student indicated that this transition was daunting because accommodating to the increased amount of reading had in turn, made it more difficult to pull information together in order to achieve an understanding:

> […] so with the academic texts, um, it's very daunting, because obviously there's these big hefty books, 600 pages and they might sort of give you two or three chapters. Like with marketing we get this and it's – read three chapters for this lecture – and the chapters are about 100 pages long.

This issue of synthesising or summarising relevant information, or identifying key points, particularly from long texts, was noted by several students. For example, a vocational student spoke about the struggles experienced when adapting to a larger volume of reading, indicating that it had been an initial barrier which went on to have repercussions in terms of both the understanding and reinterpretation of texts:

> I think this is really bad, but I feel like I've struggled more as I start the reading than the actual reading itself, if that makes sense. Because there's like so much in one chapter of a book, like you'll read one chapter of a book and it's like 10/12 pages, something like that and it's packed with a bunch of information and then you've sort of got to take time to read it, to understand it and then reinterpret it and then put it in your own words. So, I find that – like the thought of that and stuff is what I struggle with more than, you know.

In terms of writing academic essays, there was considerable variation across the student group, with some students indicating that they found this transition straightforward, with others less so. Unsurprisingly, students who had studied A-levels (including alongside a vocational qualification) which tend to involve essay writing as a typical form of disciplinary discourse felt generally well-prepared for essay writing. The subjects mentioned as enablers in this respect included English Literature, History, Geography and French. One of the FE students commented that the A-level qualification had helped them to learn to write more effectively because the required structure of an essay is always clearly provided. FE students studying both vocational qualifications and A-levels drew attention to different experiences of academic writing on the two routes: 'On my A-levels there's a way you have to write, but in BTEC […] In my A-levels you get taught the way you have to write, but in BTEC they're just like, 'write a report' and you just do it'. A different view, however, was offered by one vocational student who found that the experience of writing reports in FE was supportive at HE:

> I had a lot of experience in […] reports, because that's like the majority of my course was like that. So when it came to like writing a report I could do it without having to worry if it was in the right format.

One specific issue is the view that there are very clear expectations at university of what 'academic writing' should be and that students are not familiar with this. One student noted that, at university, essays 'have to be written more thoroughly and we'd have to do a lot more reading, so much more preparation goes into it'. Some vocational students highlighted that they felt unprepared for academic essay writing, as one student commented:

> Essays, we never really did any, so I would have liked to have done more at college, I think. Because when I did my first essay I wasn't really sure if it was along the right lines or anything. It's similar to a report in the fact that it has introduction, main body, conclusion sort of thing, but I just sort of had to guess.

Another vocational student also explained their difficulties:

> academic essays, there is an academic way of writing which you really have to follow and which is a lot different to what we're used to. It's not necessarily about knowing the content or having points to get across, it's just the way you put it down on the paper is the hardest bit.

Similarly, an A-level student described the 'shock' of becoming familiar with writing an academic essay:

[...] like back in high school the topic would be kind of like straight to the point, like at A-levels, so you know like okay I can write like 200 words, 300 words, 500 words and you're fine. But here like he said it's like 2500 words — after like two paragraphs you're like, what else can I write about this? So, it's definitely a shock, like you have to try and be more creative to try and find more stuff to write about. So definitely a challenge.

Some students discussed the importance of planning when writing academic essays, but students' testimonies of how different qualification routes had supported planning were contradictory. Some vocational students felt they had been well-prepared in this respect '[...] like coming up for a plan for the essays BTEC has helped with essay based questions, just sort of knowing the points you're going to say'. But another student, who had done both A-level and a vocational course felt that the A-level course had been more helpful than the vocational course: '[...] for A-levels they tell you to start with a plan for essays so you have a basis. So you kind of have a habit of doing it later on.' Ambiguities like this are a reminder that it is unwise to draw binary distinctions *between* qualification routes, as there are inevitably variations *within* qualification routes as well.

One aspect of academic writing which appeared to be challenging for the majority of students interviewed was referencing. A small minority, regardless of entry qualification, felt prepared and found the transition a natural progression, as noted in the comment made by a vocational student: 'referencing I've been doing the whole way through college as well, so coming to uni and referencing was pretty much like natural to me as well'. On the other hand, many students commented that previously they had had no, or very little, experience of referencing and, therefore, found it to be challenging. This perceived lack of preparation appears to be escalated by the need to learn and adapt to different referencing styles, which students represented as a 'step up' or a 'leap'. As one vocational student argued, becoming familiarised with this before entry to HE would have assisted their preparation:

> I think it would have been really useful that during BTEC or something there was more learning about different styles of referencing, because obviously there is lots of different ones [for example Harvard and APA], you can't learn the exact one you are going to be using later in life. But it would have been useful to do, like try one assignment, use this referencing and teach us about it and then do another assignment and other referencing, just learn more about it. So that would have prepared us better.

The interviews reveal, however, that some FE students were receiving guidance about referencing. One A-level English Language student felt this subject had assisted their knowledge of referencing, and another student recalled a specific session had been held at college to provide guidance about Harvard referencing. It is worth noting that all students, whether in FE or HE, and regardless of qualification route, refer to referencing simply in terms of the formatting conventions of different referencing systems. No students discussed the substantive role of citations in evidencing and justifying claims, or in locating their own work within the wider body of research in that field, suggesting a rather limited view of the role of referencing in academic writing.

The students' comments on academic literacy here reveal varying degrees of preparedness and confidence, which do appear to have some relationship to prior qualification route, but these are not straightforward. Those A-levels which involve considerable reading and extended essays to communicate understanding are evidently more aligned to conventional essay writing expectations at universities. Vocational routes do seem to place less emphasis on the writing aspect of the course, but this is equally true of A-levels which do not require extended responses or which use practical or portfolio assessments. It is important to observe here that overdependence at university level on conventional academic forms, such as the essay, may be a less inclusive practice and may contribute to the perpetuation of differential outcomes. There is a considerable body of research on academic writing, which highlights that it is 'ideologically shaped, reflecting institutional structures and relations of power' (Lillis & Tuck, 2016, p. 30), and that it does not always encompass the needs of diverse learners.

Numeracy, Mathematics and Statistics

A further transition representing a challenge for students upon entry into HE concerns the level of competence in mathematics, numeracy or statistics required by the course. This was a strong theme in the interviews but, of course, this only related to certain subjects, such as Sports Science or Business Studies which include mathematical elements in their modules. The feeling of unpreparedness seemed to be a particular problem for students who had not studied mathematics post-16, resulting in a time lapse, or 'gap' in their study of the subject. Many of the students questioned said that the study of mathematics, statistics and numeracy was a 'shock' or a 'struggle' suggesting that they did not feel confident in their mathematical ability. An A-level student who had not studied mathematics post-16 said:

> I think with numeracy skills for sure, I mean I'm familiar with all of them to a certain extent but then it's a matter of, like, it is three years ago and it's just all kind of come at once and it's kind of, I felt the lecturers were talking at us as if we already kind of knew it or were more certain of their knowledge of it. And I was literally looking at the screen and thinking I've no idea what that symbol means.

In a similar vein, a vocational student also commented:

> Yes, so statistics and stuff, because it was sort of like 'out there' and it was different for me because I have never done statistics like that if it makes sense? And then some of the modules as well, like maths and stuff. I like did my maths exam in year 10 and I never did maths again after that, so having to come back and do it again was like, whoa [laughs].

In comparison, most students with a post-16 mathematics qualification felt better prepared to study specific modules which have a 'heavy' mathematical content. As an A-level student noted: 'I chose varied A-levels, so doing maths meant that doing accountancy and quantitative methods was okay, like it was manageable because like, I had that.' However, not all students who studied mathematics post-16 reported that they felt prepared. This was illustrated by two students from different entry qualification routes who, at times, needed to seek support:

> I did AS maths so I found some of it okay and the rest a bit of a jump and I don't know, if you don't go out yourself and get help, then there's not really much there. I suppose you have to be pro-active. [A-level student]

> I don't think it is just, like BTEC students [having difficulties]. I think everyone, unless you did A-level maths, you are going to have trouble with that. And I did AS maths and I still struggle with it so – not that I did very well in my AS maths but I still, you know, have done some of the content already and I am still struggling with that. [Vocational student]

A couple of students, one vocational plus A-level, and another with a vocational qualification, stated that problems could be encountered because individuals perhaps do not have a mathematical 'brain', or 'mind'. This suggests that they view the subject as being required to be 'hard wired' in individuals, rather than something that can be learned. Other students indicated that their feeling of unpreparedness could have been eased if they had a greater understanding of the expectations involved with their degree study, as conveyed in the comments made by a vocational plus A-level student:

> but if there was some sort of warning, like we are going to slap you in the face with finance, we are going to slap you with accounting, like start getting ready with the maths. Obviously, they tell us that, but I didn't expect as much.

An A-level student also explained how their expectation changed upon entry into HE:

> Yeah for me, it was Biomechanics because after GCSE when I finished maths and physics that was it for me – like I thought I would never go back to it [laughs]. And when I came back here [to university] I realised I had to do a lot more maths and Biomechanics, so I spent most of my time going to the support sessions [with help from peer mentors] because I really struggled with maths after GCSE.

In addition, a few students expressed the view that some staff assumed that students have reached a particular level of understanding, as an A-level student said:

> I think they thought that the people who took it [the laboratory classes] assumed that everyone had a descent basic knowledge of maths. I have a basic knowledge, but GCSE maths. So, they literally sped through it and I got so lost because some of the equations, like there were so many stages to them and I had no idea what was going on.

But while many students reported difficulties, some also explained that they were able to overcome their problems by working hard to understand new course material such as statistics. In addition, a small number of students acknowledged that some teaching methods had taken into account that students might require extra support. This included the perspective of an A-level student, who said that the pace of the teaching prompted their understanding:

> [...] with some of the harder stuff in terms of maths, it started [the course] way back to GCSEs, helped our work and slowly built up to A-level and then university style. I think that was pretty helpful. And then some of the newer stuff, it was obviously phased in slowly with new concepts being introduced each week which made it much easier to understand.

A few students also talked about being taught in different groups, depending upon their mathematical background. For some modules, students were divided into those who had studied mathematics post-16 and those who had not. Whilst a few students commented that this helped them, a small number suggested that they still struggled with the mathematical content, as explained by an A-level student:

> Quantitative methods – we had an extra lecture for the non-A-level maths students that focused on the concepts and explained them in a simpler way. But I did still felt I did struggle with the maths in that. And then in terms of finance and the rest of the modules, it was just the same [for] everyone else, so I did

think it could have been slowed down a bit more for those that hadn't done A-level maths.

A small number of FE students also talked about their struggles with mathematics on their post-16 courses. Vocational students studying Business highlighted struggling with mathematics when studying accountancy and Information Communication and Technology (ICT), and one student who stated that they were 'not the best' at maths was also studying GCSE maths again, to increase their skills. Two students studying a vocational Computer Science course noted problems in class because there is a big disparity in students' mathematical background and experience. Another student noted particular difficulties with mathematics:

> when we did IT with maths and we had to look at matrices and sort of convert them and stuff, I think that was the most demanding thing and then also core maths as well which was in addition to this BTEC which was just [...] a lot quite demanding for numeracy.

As noted earlier, the students' feelings of poor preparedness for the numeracy demands of undergraduate courses was a strong theme for certain university subjects, and did not link to entry qualification so much as to whether they had continued learning mathematics post-16. Concerns about undergraduates' mathematical readiness for university study are long-standing – see for example, early concerns about mathematical readiness reported by Bell (1976) and Tall and Vinner (1981), and similar more recent studies, such as Shallcross and Yates (2014), Field (2014), and Porkess (2013). A recent report, exploring lecturers' perceptions of mathematical readiness for STEMM and Social Science degrees, suggests that the issue is less about mathematical content, and much more about new undergraduates having difficulty 'applying familiar mathematical concepts in unfamiliar contexts' (Bowyer & Darlington, 2016, p. 2). This is clearly an aspect of transition which needs further consideration both in terms of post-16 qualifications or course content in mathematics, and their parallels in undergraduate programmes.

Subject and Content Knowledge

One predictable issue in academic transition from FE to HE is that universities offer a very wide range of degree subjects, many of which are not directly paralleled by an A-level or vocational qualification. So, for example, students studying English Literature, Geography or Physics at university are highly likely to have studied A-levels in those subjects, whereas students studying Law, Business or African Studies are unlikely to have studied those subjects at A-level. As a consequence, students naturally have different transition experiences in terms of familiarity with subject content, and for some, it is the newness and distinctiveness of their chosen university degree which motivates and excites them.

However, the student interviews highlight some more nuanced ways in which the subject knowledge demands in their undergraduate programme proved challenging; and some of these challenges do relate to the different qualification routes taken prior to university. The Sports Science students in the sample included the highest proportion of students with a vocational qualification, and they were also more likely to progress successfully to year 2 than students in other subjects with a vocational qualification. Many of the Sports Science students with a vocational qualification felt that they had a well-rounded understanding of the subject of sport. But some of these students did express that they felt unprepared for the scientific subject content in their degrees, particularly Anatomy, Biology, Bioenergetics, Chemistry and Psychology. Students reported that this was a 'shock', making them feel 'behind': 'If you don't have that science background it is very hard to get on to that base level with everyone else, unless you are putting in a huge amount of work'. Many of the students with vocational qualifications found the amount of Psychology covered in the degree courses challenging:

> So, one of my best mates did Psychology at A-level and she is like, 'oh we've done this, we've done this' for almost every module, like 'we've covered this, covered that', and we feel like we're trying to play – well personally I feel I'm trying to play catch up the whole time.

Many of the difficulties associated with the Psychology content included the learning of new concepts, terminology and theories which had not been studied previously:

> [...] it is kind of the basic psychology and knowing all the different people [theorists] and things like that, that everyone's [A-level students] just had drummed into them for so long. They just know it, just like that and we don't [BTEC students], we've actually got to learn it.

Indeed, many Sports Science students with a vocational qualification felt at a disadvantage compared to A-level students when studying scientific subject knowledge. For example, one student commented on the way human physiology drew on prior knowledge: 'mainly human physiology – it's very biology and chemistry combined. And obviously people that did an A-level in biology or chemistry, they've got a humungous in-depth knowledge of chemistry and biology'. Another vocational student observed that:

> But some of my friends didn't think it would be as 'sciencey' as it was, and it shot them in the foot a little bit because they didn't put the work in, they got to the exam and then failed the exam

because they didn't [...] Okay, they didn't work, but again their base knowledge wasn't there. Whereas a lot of people can draw on what they had from A-levels.

However, difficulties with the science content were not confined to vocational students because some A-level students also explained that they had experienced similar difficulties. Central to this problem was the choice of science subject studied at A-level. For example, students who had previously studied Biology, experienced knowledge gaps for the Psychology or Chemistry content, and vice versa. A key step up was seen as the need to build upon their existing knowledge, in greater depth and at a faster pace. In addition, one A-level student went on to highlight problems raised by different examination board provision:

> I think that there's modules that you can see where even different A-levels like [...] so like AQA for PE was like really helpful for the physiology module whereas apparently OCR wasn't. Like some of my friends who did OCR PE really struggled with that module.

There was a similar set of experiences for undergraduates in Business Studies. Here students reported many difficulties with subject and content knowledge in modules such as Accountancy and Finance and this was associated with the mathematics and statistics content, as discussed previously. Many students with a vocational qualification felt well prepared for undergraduate study, stating they had a good understanding of Business and this had formed a good foundation: '[...] my college course was quite business based, so I've actually found in some areas I've actually already got prior knowledge of it'. Nevertheless, some students without an Economics A-level reported struggling with subject of Economics:

> But there was a couple like Economics [modules] which was basically if you'd done Economics A-level you wouldn't have to worry about and if you hadn't, you had no experience in it whatsoever and it was like horrific really, it was really hard.

These students' experiences do highlight the significance of subject choice post-16 in relation to degree choice, and how for some degrees some A-level choices in particular appear to be enablers. It is unlikely that there will ever be a direct alignment between FE subject choices and HE subject choices, or even that such alignment would be desirable. The diversity of courses available at university is one of the strengths of the sector and one which is attractive to students. What this inevitably means is that in those university degrees which routinely recruit students with a very diverse suite of entry qualifications, lecturers begin teaching with students at very different starting points in terms of disciplinary knowledge. This may mean that greater thought is needed in undergraduate year 1 to how the curriculum is designed to accommodate this diversity. However, bearing in mind the conclusion regarding undergraduate mathematical readiness, noted earlier, that it is the application of familiar concepts in unfamiliar settings which is the problem, it may also be important to consider whether students are drawing sufficiently on transferable skills from their post-16 disciplinary knowledge and applying that constructively to new disciplinary content at university.

Academic Support

Given some of the challenges and potential barriers to academic success at university voiced in the previous sections, it is also important to consider how these students feel about additional support available at university and how they access it.

Most students knew what support was on offer, where to find it, and for some there was a sense of being 'satisfied with the support', or that 'there was a really great support network', and these students had the attitude that if you look for help, you can find it. There were a few variables around the visibility of support between institutions, with a few feeling it was 'hidden'; that 'I didn't know where to go or who to ask'; that there needed to be more advertising because 'you have to kind of actively seek it and sort of know it's somewhere' and that 'you are told there is the maths building but unless you sort of really ask around you don't know'. However, responses also suggested that many were not accessing the available support facilities despite this awareness. Quite a few retrospectively regretted not having accessed support when they needed it as the comments following reveal:

> when I needed help I should have gone and got it.

> I'm the kind of person that tries to do it by myself and I do agree that at some point I should have accessed what was available.

> I would have probably emailed the lecturer and been like 'Listen, can you explain this to me?' [...] but yeah, that's what I should have done and could have done but [...].

The reasons, and perceived barriers, behind this were both emotional and personal. Quite a few students cited their own 'stubbornness' or 'laziness' as their reason for not accessing available support. But for some, it was more about the perception of others, and how they felt about needing support. For example, one student explained 'being scared' to ask for help; another was concerned about being thought of as 'silly'; while yet another felt it would 'be stupid of me to go and ask.' Implicit in these comments is a sense that to need support is a sign of weakness, and there is a reluctance to make this visible. For others, the unwillingness to seek or accept support was framed by a view of the importance of 'being independent' and that any academic problems could be resolved on their own through effort and hard work:

> it's not handed to you on a plate, a lot of this is how much do you want it because that's how much you're going to get out of it.

> I'm sure I can do it on my own.

> I don't think you need that much support, it's all independent and I think if you put in the time yourself then you get most out of it.

For some HE students, informal peer support, peer mentoring or buddy schemes and help from PhD students were important sources of additional support. In some cases, this stemmed from a within-cohort sense of community, shared experience and mutual support, where 'we support each other massively' and where 'for the examinations we all go through it all.' Sometimes peer support was more strategic and targeted, particularly in relation to areas students were finding problematic and where they knew someone who could help. Some of this peer support came from university friends: one student sought help from 'a friend who was in my accommodation who had done A-level maths and said he was willing to help me go through the content of the course' whilst another asked 'a friend who was from the year above me, who's already done his first year in sports science, if he could send me one of his reports just so I could see how it was written and that helped a lot'. Less commonly, the peer support was external to the university, for example, for the student who explained that 'a family friend helped me, because he works in accountancy, but it was more for the finance side'. Some of these responses show initiative and appropriate self-help strategies and perhaps contrast with the reluctance to seek more formal academic support: indeed, one student explicitly reflected that 'I found it helpful going to my friends rather than having to go to a lecturer'.

Buddy or mentor schemes available in the first year were referenced by a number of students. They were seen as optional and, if requested, a mentor was assigned, usually by email. The nature or value of the support provided was mentioned by a few and largely perceived positively. The availability of the mentor was valued: 'whenever I have needed anything, I've always just messaged my buddy and they've been able to help', as was the proactive support: 'he visited me in my halls and was really supportive and taught me how to use the library services and stuff'. Inevitably, perhaps, some peer mentors were less committed than others and at least one student noted that 'mine stopped emailing, or the group, halfway through the first year.'

In the interviews students reflected on their experiences of support from their university tutors in their first undergraduate year. For some, there was a positive acknowledgement and appreciation of the support from their tutors, with students seeing their tutor as the 'first port of call' if there was a problem, and valuing when they could 'just knock on the door', and when the tutor 'replied straight away'. The availability of the tutor was highly valued, although this does raise questions about possible unrealistic expectations of tutors and other demands on their time:

> She'd always be open and she'd make meetings outside her office hours, which I thought was a really nice approach.

> My tutors are very welcoming, if you need help they'll be there whenever you need them [...] anytime of the day or night.

> Your tutor is always there to help, which is really, really nice and that's sort of made a big difference. If we didn't have that I think it'd be hard.

In hindsight, for a few, there was a sense that not contacting their tutors when they had needed had been unwise and was something they wanted to choose in the future: 'We had the opportunity of the office hours if we need to ask questions, but I personally didn't do that this year, so I think I'll probably make more use next year.' For others, organisational barriers such as available office hour timetables were perceived as not helpful: 'I found that the office hours are really limited, that half the time I'm actually in classes or have meetings to go to.' Sometimes, even during office hours, the volume of students waiting for support was off-putting, because 'when there is a whole queue of students you might not end up asking your question' or because 'of how many people are waiting in that break time, and if you kept on asking them [the lecturers] then the students behind you would get impatient'. As a consequence, some students were less inclined to seek support and in some cases were not 'bothered every time to go to office hours'.

Some comparisons were made about the differences in the nature of tutor support post-16 and at university. One aspect of this concerned the different numbers of students for which FE and HE tutors were responsible. One student attributed the lack of personal support from tutors to the large volume of students at university recalling that 'I had more interactions with college tutors, but that's just because they have less students in the class.' A sense of having to be more proactive themselves in seeking support was also mentioned by a few: 'it's also very different because you have to make you own decision whether you want to see them or not, whereas at school it was a dedicated thing every day.' However, the strongest and most frequently noted difference between FE and HE was the nature of the relationship with tutors. More personalised contact time with tutors at FE meant they knew teachers well and built a strong relationship. For example, one student reflected that at university, in contrast to FE,

'I don't feel they have that personal connection with you to say "You could also do this". I think they just look at it and go "That's fine". Because they have so many to check I suppose'. This absence of a constructive tutor-student relationship meant that for some students seeking support was difficult because

> not having that connection there, you're a bit reluctant to ask them questions in their own time, especially if they say they could only answer questions in groups of five or something. So things like that sort of put you off.

In some cases, students felt intimidated by their tutors or found the experience of asking for tutor help difficult: 'I'd be quite worried to go up to somebody and be like "I really, really need help." Because you don't know them, so it's quite daunting'.

For a small number of students, 'not having that connection' with a tutor at HE resulted in some bad experiences. Some students felt their tutors did not know them – 'I don't think they even know my name' – and did not care about them, either academically or as an individual:

> There was nothing about how I was getting on or asking how I am, he had no records of me, no attendance or anything, there was nothing like that, he was trying to get rid of me, kind of, he didn't want me to be there.

> I was literally crying for help but he didn't care. So I wanted to swap personal tutors but I didn't know how to go about it.

For other students, the challenges of seeking tutor support related to an absence of communication. One student noted that 'I never met my personal tutor' whilst another said 'I didn't hear anything from my personal tutor or even know who it was and then I got an email after Christmas'. For others, non-response was more of an issue: 'I tried to contact mine a couple of times and they didn't respond'.

The differences in the nature of tutorial support at FE and HE, raised by the Year 1 undergraduates, is strongly reinforced in the FE student interviews, where they report very positively on the support and accessibility of tutors. One student argued 'I've got all the support I needed'; another reflected that 'You can always go and ask your teacher if you don't understand'; and another that 'teachers do communicate with us on a daily basis'. The support from FE tutors was significant in easing them through their post-16 courses, and for one student this made the 'experience a bit more relaxed and a bit less stressful'. The majority of comments about tutor support described the positive, personal and informal relationships they had developed. In part, and particularly on vocational courses, the close relationship grew out of the fact they had considerable timetabled time with their tutor. More so than with the wider range of GCSE subjects at school. As a consequence, 'it's more personal, you get to spend time with them and develop a better relationship', and with that better relationship came the sense that 'I can ask him anything in the lesson [...] it's so comfortable'. It was also evident that these students valued being treated like an adult, where the tutors 'give you a bit more respect, almost treat you like adults and don't punish you if you do something wrong'.

There were, however, FE students who were less sure of the value of the support and their relationships with the tutor. Quite naturally, where a student did not build the positive relationships with a tutor described earlier by others, it affected their willingness to seek support: 'I don't think that it helped that I didn't get on with my teacher at all. So I was more reluctant to ask for help'. More negatively, one student felt that the tutor's willingness to support was influenced by the nature of the relationship and 'if they don't like you, they don't want to help you. If you get along with them, they want to help you'. In a similar key, one student reflected that the responsibility lay with the student to establish the relationship, in a rather superficial way: 'It all comes down to how nice you are to them. A lot of people don't say that, but you have to be nice [...] for them to actually be nice back to you in work ways basically'.

What these interviews reveal is that the students' experiences of academic support in their post-16 settings and at university are diverse and complex. Most striking is the perceived difference in the nature of the relationship between tutor and student in FE and HE. In some ways, this is a natural consequence of the differences in the teaching context: in post-16 settings, students have moved from studying a broad range of subjects at GCSE with different teachers to a narrowed selection with fewer teachers in smaller groups and more timetabled time for each subject. In the case of some of the vocational courses, the students are with one tutor for most or all of the course. In universities, degree courses are much less closely linked to an individual tutor, and module choices mean that most students encounter a wide range of tutors, some for only one module course, and often in large cohorts. The post-16 setting lends itself to the establishment of close and academically supportive relationships, whereas one could argue that the university setting militates against this. At the same time, a university degree requires greater academic independence, whereas post-16 settings, particularly with the high-stakes accountability to examination results, may be tending towards greater dependency of students on tutor support. Linked to this, the students' comments on their experiences show varying degrees of self-awareness and willingness to proactively seek help, and perhaps unrealistic expectations of the amount of help and the degree of availability they expect from university tutors. These are important issues which require closer examination and further research which considers how the transition might be more effectively handled to avoid these aspects becoming barriers to progression and attainment outcomes.

Different Ways of Learning

Another theme arising from the student interviews related to their views about different ways of learning, and their experiences of differences, and similarities, in learning experiences in FE and HE. One distinctive difference, viewed positively, was the visibility of research-informed teaching at university and that 'whereas at school you just learn out of a textbook, but here they give you who's doing what research and the conclusions from that'.

One of the most commonly mentioned learning challenge for HE students was the transition to learning through lectures, and this was equally voiced, regardless of qualification route. This was frequently described as something that was challenging and requiring adjustment. Students noted the large group size of a lecture compared with the much smaller class sizes of A-level and vocational groups in the post-16 phase. This created a sense of detachment, or anonymity: one student explained that 'there's a lot of students in the lecture theatre and for some of them I don't feel I've got a connection at all; I feel like I sit there, go home and do it on my own like over the screen rather than face to face'. The heavy demands on listening were also noted: 'It was all one way, listening and you couldn't necessarily ask questions as you would do in sixth form', and a view that it was a rather passive experience where you have 'to sit there and listen' or have 'knowledge thrown at you and then you go and learn it'. Students felt that this had an effect on their capacity to learn, with some finding it 'difficult at first to even concentrate in a much larger room where you don't have that one to one support', and that 'I feel like I don't learn as much in some lectures as I could'. Students noted the variability of the quality of the lecturers, and one student specifically commented on the fast pace of learning expected in a lecture:

> the lecturer goes quite fast throughout so we have to kind of – we don't really have time to think much about what we do, it's just a really fast pace and then once we look over that and we realise we kind of get it or not.

A number of students suggested that there were fewer opportunities to ask questions and address challenging material or misconception within a lecture setting. Again, the size of the lecture was cited as the issue with some students drawing comparisons with their smaller sixth form classes.

A very small minority of students, however, were positive about lectures, with one student reflecting that 'the lectures were easy to understand'. The integration of the lecture itself with broader learning was recognised as a constructive way to learn:

> not only do they have in the PowerPoints, you've got the recordings online and they give you additional readings online. So you have got the information and you, kind of, know where to go. It's a lot more detailed, rather than at college.

Three students related positive experiences of lectures to personalities and delivery style of the lecturers. One stated that 'Some lecturers are great because they make it quite interactive' while another commented that 'you don't want to miss his lectures'. One particular lecturer was singled out for praise because he was 'absolutely amazing, every single lecture, anything we needed to read, anything that was of importance he literally broke it down for you into each section so that you could digest it'. The interaction and positive atmosphere where lecturers had a vibrant delivery style was reminiscent of their time at college for these students. More unusually, one student suggested that having some 'lecture type lessons at my school, which you just literally had to take notes from [...] helped quite a lot' in terms of preparation for university.

There were conflicting views expressed about the use of technology to support and enhance learning. Lecture-capture was discussed by a number of students. This was clearly a different approach to that experienced at FE. One student felt that the absence of recording created a stronger imperative to attend a lecture in person, whilst in contrast another student felt lecture recordings were a real benefit to learning because in a lecture:

> [...] you can't really write it down but when I'm watching them back it's pause, play, pause, play constantly. But when I'm in lectures and they say the things really fast, I can't really pick up on the majority of it.

One student bemoaned the fact that few lectures were recorded and had instead used YouTube videos as a substitute. Another student took more direct action: although her courses rarely used lecture-capture, she instead recorded them herself using her mobile phone.

The students also voiced their preferences in terms of different ways of learning, and here there were some connections between preferred ways of learning and student post-16 qualification route. Students with a vocational entry qualification were very aware of the ways of learning that their qualification had promoted and the skills they had developed:

> A lot of it was teamwork, we were allocated teams and we had to work together with people we probably wouldn't choose to. And we had to, I guess organisation skills, finding when we could meet up, finding times when we were all free to meet up and go through the group work. And in terms of the seminars, being able to have a debate, and also presentation skills.

Some of these students drew parallels between their learning experiences in FE and in HE in terms of group work and presentations. One student commented that 'we do a lot of group work, which we did a lot of in my BTEC, which I prefer a lot'. Another vocational student commented on the use of group presentations at university to promote and assess learning. She felt that this was similar to college where a 'lot of it was group work just because we were such a small group that it sort of made it easier if you all did it together'. Similarly, students with a vocational qualification commented on the use of presentations in the Business degree; and the practicals in Sports Science, with one student reflecting that 'I just prefer labs because I like getting hands on and being practical'.

Students' reflections on the different ways of learning in FE and HE, and their preferred ways of learning highlight the diversity of views about what constitutes a constructive learning environment. In general, it was not possible to determine any clear differences between students with different entry qualifications, but there was a sense that it may be the case that A-level students are appreciating more academic ways of learning and its support, whereas the students with a vocational qualification are valuing ways of learning that are consonant with their FE experience. Of course, this may be because the dominance of group work, presentations, practicals and workplace-style writing assignments are characteristic of a vocational qualification, but may be less prevalent ways of learning in university.

Conclusion

The students' articulation of how they experience learning across the transition from school/college to university are both illuminating and complex. Although there are some differences of opinion which may relate to the post-16 qualification route pursued, in general, it is hard to attribute any particular ways of learning or learning preferences firmly to qualification route. There may be some evidence that students with a vocational qualification may prefer modes of learning which involve group work, practical work and presentations because these are valued in FE; and that they may need more support with the expectations of academic literacy. But at the same time, in both of these contexts, there were A-level students who shared this tendency. Nor is it easy to discern ways of learning which act as a definitive barrier to progression for these students. Instead, the student voices sound most clearly that what one student finds supportive, another finds less so.

Nonetheless, there are some important themes emerging from this analysis of student voices across the transition. Firstly, there is a need for universities to be more aware of the multiple starting points of students on some programmes in terms of disciplinary knowledge, and to consider how to accommodate this diversity into the programme of teaching. This may be relevant to all degree courses, but may be particularly critical where a degree subject accepts students with a wide range of different A-levels or vocational subjects. Secondly, more consideration needs to be given to specific differences in ways of learning between school/FE and university, and especially a greater awareness that many students find the lecture experience challenging when they first experience it. A further strong theme concerns the nature of the relationship between students and tutors, which appears to be closer and more constructive in post-16 settings than at university. What is evident is that if universities are to meet the learning needs of a diverse student community, more active consideration needs to be given to inclusive pedagogies which are varied, or which offer more choice about the ways of learning which can be adopted to realise educational outcomes. At the same time, it is important to recognise that a university experience is not simply a replication of earlier ways of learning but one which gives greater emphasis to student independence and self-responsibility, and that this is an important aspect of a university education.

References

Bell, A. W. (1976). A study of pupils' proof-explanations in mathematical situations. *Educational Studies in Mathematics*, *7*(1), 23–40.

Bowyer, J., & Darlington, E. (2016). *"Applications, applications, applications". Lecturers' perceptions of students' mathematical preparedness for STEMM and social science degrees*. Cambridge: Cambridge Assessment.

Field, A. P. (2014). *Skills in mathematics and statistics in psychology and tackling Transition*. York: Higher Education Academy.

Lillis, T., & Tuck, J. (2016). A critical lens on writing and reading in the academy. In K. Hyland & P. Shaw (Eds.), *The Routledge handbook of English for academic purposes* (pp. 30–43). London: Routledge.

Neeley, S. D. (2005). *Academic literacy*. New York, NY: Longman.

Porkess, R. (2013). *A world full of data. Statistics opportunities across A-level subjects*. London: Royal Statistical Society/The Institute and Faculty of Actuaries.

Shallcross, D. E., & Yates, P. (2014). *Skills in mathematics and statistics in chemistry and tackling transition*. York: Higher Education Academy.

Tall, D., & Vinner, S. (1981). Concept image and concept definition in mathematics with particular reference to limits and continuity. *Educational Studies in Mathematics*, *12*(2), 151–169.

Chapter 5

Assessment Practices: Student Voices on Their Experiences of Assessment across the Transition

Debra Myhill and Rebecca Morris

Introduction

The previous chapter explored student perspectives on their teaching and learning experiences across the FE-HE transition, and some of the challenges they faced as a consequence. In this chapter, we explore students' reflections and observations, captured from the same set of interview data. The topic of assessment merits a separate chapter as the students were very vocal about it, and with divergent views. Assessment inevitably provokes strong responses from students because it is so directly linked to attainment outcomes, and in the context of a book which is examining differential outcomes for students from different qualification routes, it is axiomatically significant.

There is, of course, a substantive body of research on the importance of assessment for learning, or formative assessment which is generic to all learning contexts and settings (see, for example, Black & William, 1998, 2009; Hattie, 2009; Hattie & Timperley, 2007). This research distinguishes between summative assessment, which determines the level of attainment achieved in an assignment or examination, and formative feedback which is intended to inform the learner of their achievements and learning needs, as well as to inform the teacher about how future teaching may need to be adapted to support identified learning needs. Thus formative assessment is intrinsically related to the possibility of improvement in learning, and learning gains in outcomes. Nicols and Macfarlane (2006, p. 204) argue, however, that the research on formative assessment appears to have had 'much less influence on higher education'. It is also the case that in the annual National Student Survey, which seeks students' evaluation of the quality of their learning experiences, the questions related to Assessment score badly for many universities. In 2018, for example, assessment and feedback was the lowest scoring strand of the survey (73% satisfaction) related to learning, with only satisfaction with the Students' Union being lower (OfS, 2018). And yet, there is an extensive and international research literature in Higher Education, with one highly rated journal *Assessment and Evaluation in Higher Education* devoted exclusively to this area. Thus, understanding the nature of the assessment experiences that students encounter, their assessment preferences and their responses to assessment is crucial to understanding differential outcomes.

Assessment Preferences

The students in our study voiced varying perspectives on their preferred modes of assessment, and there were some differences which linked, in part at least, to entry qualification. In the HE cohort, some students expressed a strong preference for coursework essays as opposed to examinations, and students with vocational entry qualifications were more likely to be in this group. This almost certainly links with their FE experience where the BTEC places greater emphasis on coursework than A-level or IB. However, the differences between vocational and A-level entry routes were not binary, and there were also A-level students who also preferred coursework essays. In general, this was because students felt their strengths lay in coursework essay writing rather than examinations, as they could demonstrate more clearly what they knew or understood through this mode. Typical comments included:

> [I am] more accustomed to this – if I work for an independent essay, I get more information than if I study for an exam'. (A-level plus vocational student)

> I am able to get across what I understand better than in an exam. (Vocational student)

> This was my preferred way of work. (A-level student)

One vocational student, however, nuanced this preference slightly differently by noting that they would 'rather do a 10–20 minute presentation than write an essay as [I'm] better at speaking than writing'. This contrasts with previous comments which were largely about the way examinations, with time constraint and question constraints, are harder to demonstrate learning than coursework essays for which students can better prepare and have time for revision and reflection. This student's comment draws attention to a different assessment binary, that of oral and written modes.

These comments regarding a preference for coursework essays aligns with a general view preferring coursework to examinations for a significant proportion of the students. For students who had experienced coursework in their post-16 learning, there was a sense of familiarity and preparedness and being better at it than examinations: 'we had coursework for our A-levels, we understand how the coursework here works as well as trying to meet the deadlines because we had many of these'. One student preferred 'the coursework element much more because it's easier to prepare for' whilst another student felt that coursework helps to 'boost up grades because every module has either 15% to 20% coursework'. Some students had made a deliberate choice post-16 to choose courses with more coursework because they felt better able to demonstrate their learning through coursework. As one student reflected, 'I changed from A-level to BTEC because of the coursework based element and I'm terribly bad at writing essays and the exam environment'. One student directly raised the issue of fairness, challenging the dominance of examinations as a mode of assessment: 'I'm better at coursework than examinations, so to be judged on examinations alone to get into a good university isn't fair.' There were students, however, who felt more comfortable with examination assessments, again because of the nature of their assessment experiences in FE:

> A-level maths was examinations, the maths that we are doing here is coursework […] which I find a bit weird because I'm not used to doing maths and coursework together […] in terms of coursework I was a bit lost.

In general, the FE cohort were much more inclined to express preferences for coursework than examination, and their views largely echoed those made by the students in HE. They felt they could demonstrate 'more progress with this assessment model than examinations' and that they 'broke down the exam pressure as don't have to worry about revision'. They also felt that it was 'more practical […] more time to find information' and that when given a brief 'it was easier to follow and less pressure'.

Changes in Assessment Experiences across the FE-HE Transition

Students' comments about their assessment preferences relate strongly to what they know and are familiar with, as voiced above, and a cluster of comments from the students related to challenges they had experienced in relation to different assessment experiences in their FE and HE settings. There were some generally occurring themes around transitional experiences relating to: feeling prepared when asked to engage in known assessment practices such as giving presentations, or writing essays; a lack of revision skills and how to manage revision; no experience of examinations for vocational students; and barriers to accessing support from tutors.

Because A-levels, the IB and vocational qualifications have differing assessment modes, students' reflection on assessment experiences across the transition inevitably reflected their post-16 experience. Some students with vocational entry qualifications, or both vocational and A-level qualifications, felt their chosen educational path had prepared them well for university, including some students who believed they were better prepared for transition than their A-level peers:

> [...] I agree with the juggling all the coursework assignments at once. I've noticed that A-level people have found that quite difficult, so I think for us we're just used to doing it.
>
> What I've noticed like as a BTEC there was more of a variety of assessment methods so I did a lot of presentations as well as essays and like one to one interviews. Lots of people who did A-Levels did like essays and then it was examinations, so for me personally I feel better prepared for a lot of the assessment methods.
>
> [...] with having coursework now and having examinations as well, it's kind of easy for me because I sort of did that in college anyway because I did like a BTEC with an A-Level.

The giving of presentations was widely referred to by vocational students as a familiar form of assessment from FE to HE. The sense of confidence with this type of assessment came across as reassuring to many, one making the contrast that they felt 'more prepared than some of my friends that did A-level who haven't done presentations before [...] I had 2 years preparation'. Another said that 'I already had those sort of skills constantly in the back of my mind so I think that helped me compile the presentations and actually do it [...] I don't mind it as much as if I'd never done them before', whilst another noted that 'surprisingly I find presenting work easier, I'm quite confident when I'm in a group'. There seemed to be a recognition that a diversity of assessment practices meant that everybody could play to their own strengths. In particular, having both presentational and written modes of assessment was noted as a positive. One A-level student, commenting on enjoying the mix of assessment practices, reflected that 'obviously some people can be really good at presentation and some people can really not like talking in front of people whereas they can be really good at writing a long essay'. One student, however, did feel that there was a challenge particular to group presentation forms of assessment: 'it was actually quite difficult to adapt to actually putting your work together in a big group to make it all sound like one person's written it'.

Many students had something to say about examinations, but for the vocational students who had had no examinations on their post-16 courses, they were understandably a particular challenge. Some observed that having 'not done any for 2 years [...] getting back into it was difficult', and that '[...] a lot of worry came from the fact that we were assessed on examinations, especially by the fact that I did BTEC where it was all essay written'. Another student noted the difficulty caused by the pressure of speed in an examination, compared with coursework essays: 'you're used to writing essays, you have more time for research whereas with examinations like you have to work much faster'. Linked to this was inexperience or uncertainty about how to prepare for examinations:

> First of all in semester one I didn't do very well in my examinations, but I did quite well in the coursework, in semester two I've done well-ish on the coursework, but I think obviously after getting my results back from semester one I'm like revising a lot more, so like preparing myself a lot more.

> After I had my examinations, I was a bit shocked at having examinations, so I've tried to be a lot more prepared, so I'm not so stressed.

One aspect of examination preparation which the vocational students discussed was revision, and a lack of confidence with revision skills, leading one student to reflect that 'I think probably some revision skills sessions, that would have been really useful. Particularly for us who haven't actually been doing revision like for the last two years.' For others, the issue was more about the lack of explicit direction about what to revise:

> It was a bit tough because we didn't get a lot of direction on it, like a lot of lecturers will be like, 'Focus your revision on such and such', but for anatomy it wasn't like that, it was very much, 'Go away and revise'. There was no direction. So what we all thought would come up in the exam didn't.

Students who had experienced examinations in post-16 felt they had been better prepared at FE than in HE. Sometimes, this was caused by a perceived lack of explicit information about examination structure in HE, recognising that 'knowing some structure, what is actually needed, will help the exam. The coursework I'm not too worried, because you have a task list [...] but for the exam you don't have a clue what you're doing'. At the same time, some students had expected to receive revision lists, based on previous experience of being 'given a sort of list, maybe not the questions that are going to be asked, but definitely a list that'll help you to answer questions'. Other students were surprised at the lack of information about how to be successful in examination questions, recalling that at FE 'you'd have almost a tick list of what you needed to be mentioning to get that band. And for here you don't have anything like that.' The use of past papers was also mentioned as a contrast between FE and HE, with one student noting that 'it'd really help if they could put up a lot of past papers, like potential ones, or prospective ones for us to like have proper practice. Some vocational students felt examples as models had been useful at college: 'you'd get given an example piece of work, on a different topic but so you knew what sort of thing, how it had to be laid out. But here, it wasn't that here, and

I struggled a little bit'. Finally, concern for a few focused around the amount of reading preparation required for examinations, with the view that it was:

> a big leap from going to A-Levels to how much independent reading we have to do for uni as well because the reading lists are sometimes so long and it's difficult to know exactly what you need to remember for like the examinations.

Even for A-level students who were familiar with examinations, the type of examination was relevant. In particular, multiple-choice assessment received mixed responses in terms of adjusting to transition expectations. One student reflected that 'I'm a bit thrown by them, because we didn't have them at A-level or GCSE really. The closest you'd get to that really was a one-liner. One line answer' and another admitted that multiple-choice question examinations were 'tougher to be honest because, like hardly any MCQs in A-level, and here like it's 45 marks, 50?' In contrast, some students enjoyed the new experience of multiple-choice questions and was 'thankful for MCQs at least there isn't that whole, you know, when you get a question wrong you deduct a mark, so thankful for that. It's a plus'.

Adapting to Changed Assessment Expectations across the FE-HE Transition

Both FE and HE students were in contexts where they had had to adapt to potentially different patterns and processes in assessment, as they moved either from GCSE assessment practice to those in post-16 programmes, or from post-16 to undergraduate year 1. In their interviews, students shared both objective experiences around what assessment practices they had encountered to more subjective, and more nuanced responses around adapting to assessment practices. The HE students observed that at university they had experienced a 'whole variety of everything', including computer-based tests, multiple-choice examinations or short answers, practical assessments, coursework, group work assessments, presentations, and written examinations. When exploring their comments in more detail, it was apparent that there was a strong sense from many students, regardless of entry qualification, that there had been no real shared understanding of what they should expect around the whole issue of assessment before coming to university. Before arriving at university they did not know, for example, the structure or style of examinations; the mark schemes and grading of examinations and coursework; or the revision skills necessary. One student summarised this by reflecting that, in addition to the standard information given about their course, they wanted:

> the examination expectations of each individual module and I'd like to know whether it's going to be multiple choice, whether it's going to be coursework essays expected and whether in those

examinations whether it's going to be based on particular texts or whether it's you're expected to do further reading.

This sense of 'not knowing' what was expected was apparent regardless of the assessment method, or the entry qualification route, and showed how uncertain students felt about the assessment criteria and expectations:

> I feel like an exam's gone okay but then again I feel like actually I don't know how they're going to mark it. I may think I've got a good structure but they might not.

> [...] my essay was just tricky because you've got no idea what they expect from you.

> So like for the beginning when we started our coursework [...] that is when I was struggling because I didn't know what to do, what were they expecting from us.

Several students referred specifically to the absence of a mark scheme: one student observed that 'you hope that you are answering the question properly because there is not a mark scheme in some cases' whilst another similarly commented that ' [...] you don't know what the topics are, what the questions are going to be, because that would be cheating, so having that mark scheme would have been helpful for that so we're not completely lost'. These comments may indicate a specific area of assessment where students find adapting to HE practices difficult. University assessment processes are governed by strict quality assurance processes and assessment criteria should be made clear to students. But there may be a dissonance here between HE and FE, where post-16 examinations have very clear mark schemes for each award band, often matched with exemplars showing how particular responses earn particular marks. One student noted that grading schemes at university are different, but not necessarily less helpful: 'some of the grading schemes are just, they are different like with JAVA I had a really interesting grading scheme for the coursework compare to the exam'. Some students were aware of a trajectory of adaptation and adjustment over time:

> I think I have adapted to it [assessment practices] much better in the second semester because I knew what they were looking for and how they're marking compared to the first semester where I had no idea.

There are very strong parallels in the FE cohort, describing how they adapted to post-16 practices compared with GCSE. These are a salient reminder that it may be changes in practices which are the key factor, not necessarily university assessment practices. There was a sense that the vocational students were clearer about assessment criteria than A-level students, as the two comments below illustrate:

> It has been quite easy because the input that we've been given is really easy and the tutor's helped us out as well with each assignment and we get a lot of input on how to do the assignment and what criteria we're trying to achieve.

> When you do AS levels they don't really break down where we can get the marks, whereas with BTECs we have the power to get distinctions because it clearly breaks down what criteria we need to meet, so I think it's much easier to do our assignments because we know what we have to achieve, whereas in AS levels we don't have that, we're just guessing what we think we have to write.

With regard to developing as a learner from their first year to the second year, some students in FE, like their HE counterparts, felt their understanding of assessment processes and expectations developed over time:

> By the end of the second year we know how to get the grades that we want to get, which is good because I think the first year was trial and error and I didn't really know what grades I was getting, like how important they were for university.

> I found it difficult in the first year getting all the information into like one report and then as the year went by I started knowing what information was relevant to my assignments, so I had to just cut it through and it ended up a good piece of work.

And for many students, there was the new experience that once an assignment had been submitted, the outcome was final with no resubmission opportunities, in contrast with college experiences:

> [...] before we were used to – let's say I got a 60 at college it would have been a thing like you get a resubmission, [...] here it's whatever you get, that's what you get back. So you don't get second chances.

Feedback on Assessment

The issue of the nature and helpfulness of feedback given on assessments in HE was the most strongly voiced theme relating to assessment, and there were few significant differences between students groups which related to the kind of entry qualification they possessed. Assessment feedback has been defined as 'all feedback exchanges generated within assessment design, occurring within and beyond the immediate learning context, being overt or covert (actively and/or passively sought and/or received) and, importantly, drawing from a range of sources' (Evans, 2013, p. 71). Havnes, Smith, Dysthe, and Ludvigsen (2012) argue, having reviewed different researcher perspectives on feedback, that there is 'one common trait: the focus is on the provision of feedback and characteristics of the feedback as information provided mainly to the learner' (Havnes et al., 2012, p. 21). In light of this, students' expressions of how helpful they find feedback at university is a valuable mirror on the efficacy of current HE assessment feedback practices. In general, the students in our study were not positive about their university experiences of assessment feedback, particularly in relation to how effectively it enabled them to learn from the feedback to inform future effort.

With regard to using feedback for the process of feed-forward in improving their work, many students, regardless of entry qualification, felt there was a lack of constructive feedback after examinations. For some students, a consequence of this was that they found it hard to know how well they were progressing or what they needed to improve. Sometimes, this was because the only feedback received was summative, in the form of a mark or grade, so as one student reflected 'you don't really know where you've gone wrong. So hard to know how to improve'. This desire to understand how to improve was a strong common theme:

> We were assessed on four different areas and it was just marks more than actual where you went wrong and what we could have done better.

> I wish they'd put some of the answers- read them up [...] so we would do the exam but we wouldn't know if we're getting it right or wrong.

> I think post-examinations [...] it would be good to have a lecture where your lecturer just goes through where people made the majority of mistakes. Just so then you can learn from it, because otherwise you get your paper back and you got this percentage but you don't actually know where you went wrong on it. So it's hard to know where your knowledges actually are.

> They might end up ticking the whole thing but they might still only give you 50% and you're like you've ticked the whole thing but why it's only 50%? So you'd want to know why the mark's been awarded or why it hasn't been awarded or how could it be improved.

Equally, many students were disappointed with the amount and quality of written feedback on coursework assignments. Some students found their feedback lacked detail: 'I expected it to be more detailed, much more detailed actually. I think it would have helped'. Others found their feedback 'a bit vague, like I've had feedback like your structure's not very good and it's like, where do I go from there?' Still others found it inconsistent from assignment to assignment: 'sometimes I have been given three paragraphs worth of feedback, but another time I have been given one line'.

The process or format of how feedback was delivered was commented by some as being less personal than they had experienced post-16. Some students felt they were missing on-to-one feedback, or oral feedback or that when given, it was more generic than specific and individual. One student made a direct comparison of assessment feedback across the transition: 'Feedback from university is by email and then feedback at school was obviously one-to-one. So I found it easier to gauge what I had to improve when it was on-to-one'. Another student expressed regret at the absence of one-to-one feedback:

> With essays and presentations that's within a little seminar you would get a little sheet with what you've done well and stuff. But that was still not one-to-one talking [...] I did miss that because you don't really know what you can improve on really.

Some students felt there were inconsistencies between lecturers in terms of the amount of feedback, with the consequence that 'some lecturers were really informative and said what you did well and not so well, whereas other lecturers didn't really give you much feedback'. There was also some concern expressed about the consistency of assessment judgements made, as reflected in marks, and poor feedback on why that mark had been allocated:

> I was given exactly the same mark and only had feedback on one piece of the work that I did and every time I went to query it, he couldn't actually justify why I had the mark [...] I found that very frustrating because of the amount of work I'd put into the module and I couldn't see myself improving on the course.

> Well, I've had identical feedback to one of my friends but we got different marks so that was a bit shocking because we were working in a group but we had to submit something individually and we had exactly the same comments.

In other situations, the problem relates more to the clarity of expression in the feedback:

> Some lecturers they'll comment on it (assignment) and they'll write like in full sentences and you can understand what they're trying to say. Other ones will use almost a different language it

seems and you'll go like what does it mean? And you'll read it ten times and still I don't know what it means.

Another issue mentioned by a few was around the delay in receiving their work back, which meant that when the feedback is provided it has less impact on improving work because 'you've moved on and have got other things to worry about'. There is a clear sense here that students see feedback in a rather mature way, not simply as feedback on what they have achieved but as feedforward for what they might do in the future. One student showed clearly this wish to use assessment feedback to inform future learning:

> especially if you're sort of doing two courseworks overlapping and you've got feedback from one of them while you're still doing the other [...] you'd be like, I can apply this to this coursework [...] rather than waiting three, four weeks later getting it back and then I can't remember what it was about.

For some students, these university experiences of feedback contrasted with what they had typically experienced in FE: 'In college the feedback would be pretty much immediate [...] whereas at uni it's sort of, you hand it in and you wait weeks and weeks to hear back.'

For a couple of students from vocational routes, receiving feedback had been a negative experience, even dispiriting and had made them question both their ability and their educational decisions:

> I had an assignment and it had 80 comments on it and one of them was positive and the rest was this is wrong, this is wrong, this is wrong [...] it was really disheartening because I was like [...] maybe I can't actually do this.

> It was so disheartening because it was like one of the first assignments and it was right at the start of the year and you're like, oh my gosh, I've done BTEC and I can't write because I didn't do a good enough course, I didn't do A-Levels. I should have done A-Levels.

There were, however, some students who were more positive about their experience of assessment feedback. In general, the positive responses were a direct inverse of students' dissatisfaction, particularly commenting that the feedback had helped them understand how to improve:

> For the second one [piece of coursework] we got basic feedback online based on rubrics that it was marked on, we got to know

> which band it was [...] it was useful as it showed the different areas and how you scored, so you' know how to improve for next time.

> The coursework that we've got back they've written stuff down, I think that's useful because you realise where you've gone wrong [...] they give a paragraph looking at each part of your work.

> They like ticked what we did well and what we didn't do well, so looking back at the first one and improving for the next one.

As a consequence of constructive feedback, one student was able to argue that 'I've improved my grade on all three [essays]. So yeah, the feedback for me has been quite valuable.' Another student noted the value of module feedback which taken different forms, including firstly 'a general feedback' to the whole group, but accompanied by an invitation for individuals to see the tutor to 'go through it' if they wanted to. This student had followed this up with a short face to face meeting and found the tutor had helpfully 'written all over my script' which had 'been useful for other modules as well'.

The FE students in the sample reported largely positive responses to the feedback they had received on their post-16 courses. Some students made direct comparisons to how feedback at college was more detailed than at school and more individualised. Crucially, the feedback was seen to facilitate progress in their grades because the 'corrections from my teachers also helped so you could go through the course and get good grades' – the opposite of the experiences of many of the HE students. Typically, students reported that:

> They look specifically at your work, rather than in school it's more of a general class thing [...] individual, so we can build on our work, which helps us get the higher grades basically.

> Feedback is really detailed and it's not just like one sentence, it's more like a little chunk where you know what you've done and what you've done right and wrong. And how you could improve if you were to do it again.

One particular student went further and praised the effort made by their teacher to mark their work:

> Because we spend hours on our assignments and it's nice to know they also spend time to read through each bit and make sure that they mark it they give good feedback rather than just a couple of lines [...] which is really helpful.

There were, of course, some students who felt in certain instances, feedback was less detailed and therefore less helpful:

> I would say everyone who gets feedback does have to speak to the teacher, even if they receive the feedback on email because about half the things you don't understand how you've done it wrong.

> Some of our lecturers when they marked, it was generic, like, 'For it to pass put in more detail on a certain topic,' it wasn't more specific on what we needed to include. And some we didn't actually get verbal feedback, it was just put on Moodle you get a feedback sheet.

Conclusion

Reflecting on the perspectives voiced by these students, there are two clear themes which merit some further discussion, namely the types of assessment and the helpfulness of assessment feedback. In general, in post-16 programmes, there is more diversity in types of assessment on the vocational courses than there is in A-levels, as the political mandates in recent years have shifted the emphasis to terminal examination assessments. There is also diversity in types of assessment in university undergraduate programmes, and these vary from subject to subject. From the testimonies of students in our sample, there are some subjects which still rely very heavily on examinations; in general, written modes of assessments, particularly essays, dominate. The students' voices reveal that, unsurprisingly, students do not share a consensus around what kind of assessment is preferred, reflecting the diversity of previous learning experiences and personal predilections. For universities seeking to reduce differential outcomes, it seems likely that a positive way forward would be to ensure that students do experience a diversity of assessment types, including a reduction in reliance on examination and the written essay, and that this diversity is reflected more consistently within programmes as well as across an institution. This would reduce any inbuilt assessment biases which derive from the nature of students' post-16 assessment experiences. Linked to this, it may be helpful to be more explicit about the particular learning value of different types of assessment: for example, that academic essays develop strong argumentation skills, and that examinations test what learning can be recalled and used under time pressure; however, presentations develop the capacity to communicate concepts and arguments to a more public audience, and group assessments determine teamworking capacities. Equally, thought and professional discussion might reflect on how all these forms of assessment can be equally robust and intellectually rigorous, to avoid rather banal hierarchies of assessment types. In this way, the use of diverse types of assessment is all complementary to a rich learning experience, and to the roundedness of the education with which students engage.

The issue of the helpfulness of assessment feedback is a more thorny issue, and from the voices of the students here, one which is significant. Yet the research on assessment feedback in Higher Education offers a relatively consistent view of the characteristics of effective feedback:

> Good feedback practice:
>
> - helps clarify what good performance is (goals, criteria, expected standards);
> - facilitates the development of self-assessment (reflection) in learning;
> - delivers high-quality information to students about their learning;
> - encourages teacher and peer dialogue around learning;
> - encourages positive motivational beliefs and self-esteem;
> - provides opportunities to close the gap between current and desired performance;
> - provides information to teachers that can be used to help shape teaching.
>
> *Source*: Nicols and Macfarlane (2006, p. 205)

In the past 20 years, universities have become significantly more transparent about their assessment criteria and standards, including the development of national subject benchmarks. And yet students still do not find assessment feedback valuable. Rust, Price, and O'Donovan (2003) have argued that 'the continued emphasis on explicit articulation of assessment criteria and standards is not sufficient to develop a shared understanding of 'useful knowledge' between staff and students' (2003, p. 162); instead they maintain more attention needs to be given to developing shared understanding through discussion and socialisation. In a similar vein, Boud and Malloy (2013) suggest that assessment and feedback need to become more learned-centred, requiring a 'repositioning' of the competencies needed by teachers such that they become:

> designers and sustainers of the learning milieu; establishing conditions in which students can operate with agency. The focus of sustainable feedback shifts from the provision of feedback to the design of learning environments, the seeding of generative tasks and the fostering of interactions with and between students and staff. (Boud & Malloy, 2013, p. 720)

Other researchers (Huisman, Saab, van den Broek, & van Driel (2019); Nicol, Thomson, & Breslin, 2013) draw attention to the value of peer and self-assessment in developing more grounded shared understanding. Two recent meta-analyses of peer feedback in Higher Education highlight their potential. Nicol et al. (2013) argued that being involved in peer review involves the student reviewer in a range of evaluative judgements, and prompts reflection not just on peers' work but on the students' own. Because peer feedback requires the understanding and application of assessment criteria, it can also reduce students' reliance on external, tutor-led feedback.

However, the students' dissatisfaction with the feedback they receive may not be simply related to the quality of the feedback provided at university. The contrast between FE and HE assessment experiences were strong, and then further amplified by differences in FE assessment practices in A-level and vocational routes. There seems little doubt that post-16 students tend to receive more feedback, more individualised feedback and more feedback aligned to clearly defined performance standards. This may be more attributable to the high accountability culture in FE than to superior professional understanding of effective feedback. The school sector in England is currently heavily driven by a high-stakes assessment culture because of the direct accountability placed on schools and FE colleges relating to their assessment results. This is true across primary, secondary and post-16 phases, but the problem is neatly summarised in a recent report by the House of Commons Education Committee (HCEC) looking particularly at primary education, which concluded that 'the high stakes system can negatively impact teaching and learning, leading to narrowing of the curriculum and "teaching to the test", as well as affecting teacher and pupil wellbeing' (HCEC, 2017, p. 3). Instead, they recommended that assessment should be 'a diagnostic tool to help teachers identify pupils' needs and must avoid shifting negative consequences of high stakes accountability' (HCEC, 2017, p. 3). Concerns about the effect of high-stakes assessment on the quality of learning is not confined to England: similar concerns have been voiced in research from the United States (Resnick & Schantz, 2017), from Israel (Klein, 2017) and from Australia (Polesel, Rice, & Dulfer, 2014). Assessment is somewhat less high-stakes in the university sector, though degree outcome measures are used as performance indicators to compare universities.

The stance expressed by many students in our study was that they wanted feedback to be more like their post-16 experiences, with some sense that they expected rather precise information about what topics/examination questions might be, and very direct guidance on what to do to get better grades. This may reflect a mismatch of expectations between students at university and their lecturers and raises important questions about what kind of learners universities are aspiring to foster, and perhaps how universities might support students from a rather dependency-driven assessment culture move to a more independent, self-directed engagement with learning and assessment. In the words of one lone voice in our study – 'it's a different style you've got to get used […] It's just, sort of, a lot more independent'.

References

Black, P., & Wiliam, D. (1998). Assessment and classroom learning. *Assessment in Education: Principles, Policy, Practice, 5*(1), 7–74.

Black, P., & Wiliam, D. (2009). Developing the theory of formative assessment. *Educational Assessment, Evaluation and Accountability, 21*, 5–31.

Boud, D., & Molloy, E. (2013). Rethinking models of feedback for learning: The challenge of design. *Assessment & Evaluation in Higher Education, 38*(6), 698–712.

Evans, C. (2013). Making sense of assessment feedback in higher education. *Review of Educational Research, 83*(1), 70–120.

Hattie, J. A. (2009). *Visible learning. A synthesis of over 800 meta-analyses related to achievement.* New York, NY: Routledge.

Hattie, J., & Timperley, H. (2007). The power of feedback. *Review of Educational Researcher, 77*(1), 81–112.

Havnes, A., Smith, K., Dysthe, O., & Ludvigsen, K. (2012). Formative assessment and feedback: Making learning visible. *Studies in Educational Evaluation, 38*, 21–27.

HCEC (House of Commons Education Committee). (2017). *Primary assessment.* London: House of Commons. Retrieved from https://publications.parliament.uk/pa/cm201617/cmselect/cmeduc/682/682.pdf

Huisman, B., Saab, N., van den Broek, P., & van Driel, J. (2019). The impact of formative peer feedback on higher education students' academic writing: A Meta-Analysis. *Assessment and Evaluation in Higher Education, 44*(6), 863–880.

Klein, J. (2017). How schools cope with the double challenge of excellence in high-stakes risk tests and investment in education. *Assessment in Education: Principles, Policy & Practice, 24*(4), 474–488.

Nicol, B., Thomson, A., & Breslin, C. (2013). Rethinking feedback practices in higher education: A peer review perspective. *Assessment and Evaluation in Higher Education, 39*(1), 102–122.

Nicols, D. J., & Macfarlane, D. (2006). Formative assessment and self-regulated learning: A model and seven principles of good feedback practice. *Studies in Higher Education, 31*(2), 199–218.

OFS. (2018). *National Student Survey.* Retrieved from https://www.officeforstudents.org.uk/advice-and-guidance/student-information-and-data/national-student-survey-nss/

Polesel, J., Rice, S., & Dulfer, N. (2014). The impact of high-stakes testing on curriculum and pedagogy: A teacher perspective from Australia. *Journal of Education Policy, 29*(5), 640–657.

Resnick, B. L., & Schantz, F. (2017). Testing, teaching, learning: Who is in charge? *Assessment in Education: Principles, Policy & Practice, 24*(3), 424–432. doi:10.1080/0969594X.2017.1336988

Rust, C., Price, M., & O'Donovan, B. L. (2003). Improving students' learning by developing their understanding of assessment criteria and processes. *Assessment and Evaluation in Higher Education, 28*(2), 147–164.

Chapter 6

Students' Voiced Experiences of Social Transitions: Facilitating a Sense of Belonging

Helen Mackenzie and Rebecca Morris

Introduction

The transition for young people from school or college into Higher Education (HE) can be viewed as being multiple and concurrent. It involves, for example, a change in context such as leaving home for the first time and perhaps moving to a different town or city, at the same time as becoming familiar with a university campus, alongside a move to a new education system. In the previous two chapters, students' experiences of ways of learning, including various academic transitions, and their experiences of assessment were presented. This chapter builds upon this by shedding light on a number of transitions associated with students' social experiences. This is a key part of the student experience to investigate because academic and social transitions are inevitably intertwined and whilst there is usually no single reason why students might consider dropping out of university, a lack of social integration can play a crucial role (see Jones, 2008). This view connects to the discussion presented in Chapter 2 which highlighted that a sense of belonging and the development of multiple, social and learner identities, can be significant in assisting the facilitation of successful transitions for different students, including non-traditional students and those with vocational qualifications.

Many educational studies have revealed that a feeling of belonging and 'fitting in' can be central to fostering academic success including retention, attainment and learner engagement (see, for example: Braxton, Milem, & Sullivan, 2000; Maestas, Vaquera, & Munoz Zehr, 2007; Mountford-Zimdars et al., 2015; Thomas, 2012; Tinto, 1998; Yorke & Longden, 2004). A sense of belonging is often seen as involving a feeling of identification with others and the forming of social bonds. This view is based upon the human need for affiliation which the psychologist Abraham Maslow (1968) described as being one of the necessary requirements to lead to physical, emotional, behavioural and mental well-being. However, if a sense of belonging is not satisfied, it could be associated with the feeling of negative emotions such as stress and anxiety as well as feelings of social isolation, loneliness and alienation (Baumeister & Leary, 1995) which could potentially impact adversely upon students' various transitions. As highlighted in Chapter 2, the student cohort who take vocational qualifications are more likely to share the characteristics of the widening participation cohort for example, by their ethnic and socio-economic background. In addition, it was forwarded that some student groups can be viewed as being more different than others hence positioned as 'outsiders' by traditional education institutions. Therefore, a sense of belonging might be an important influence in shaping students' social transitions as well as acting as a useful heuristic to explore the ways that students, as well as those with vocational qualifications, might feel at odds within an institutional culture.

This chapter puts three main themes concerning students' social transitions under the spotlight and in so doing examines the key facilitators and possible hindrances that students might experience. It begins with an exploration of the various issues surrounding students' social networks with peers and friendship groups. First-year university students' choices concerning their accommodation are also considered, before moving briefly to outline students' involvement with clubs, societies and team activities on campus.

Social Networks

This particular aspect of students' voiced experiences captures the nature and extent of these students' social networks, plus the types of networks students are involved in. The quality of their social experiences and friendship groups is also explored.

To begin, an examination of the experiences of Further Education (FE) students studying vocational qualifications at college revealed that some students had built strong friendship groups and good peer relationships which were found to be supportive. As one student reflected, 'my group, we've been really strong this year, we've been there for each other. And I think that group atmosphere, being all together and being able to work with each other, really helps'. These relationships assisted the establishment of stable friendships in which, 'we're all very close, we're all pretty much really good friends' and where 'we have a lot of banter, a lot of *funny* times with each other, and I think we've grown to really like each other'. This, in turn, leads to the formation of academically supportive peer groups where:

> we also help each other out, when we have an assignment if somebody's struggling, we all go over, make sure they're all right, help them out in any way that we can.

In some cases, it was helpful that the friendship groups had been partly pre-established because:

> a lot of us knew each other before, I knew at least four of them because I'd danced with them all. So, a lot of us knew each other, knew of each other, so we just clicked straight away.

For other students, initial concerns about being with a different group of people and making friends were overcome by the friendliness of the group: 'I get quite bad anxiety about classrooms and especially going into new places, but it was a very smooth transition, very welcoming'. Therefore, it seems that becoming personally accepted, included and supported by others within the FE college classroom has fostered a sense of belonging which can also result in assisting academic engagement (see Goodenow, 1993).

However, it was also clear that not all groups were equally as strong. Some vocational students' comments suggested that their friendship groupings at college were, in contrast, quite restricted. One student said, 'we don't come in to like talk to everyone. We only talk to people that we know', and another in the same focus group commented, 'we only speak to who comes in to the lesson'. There also appeared to be stronger connections within the subject group, rather than wider college groups, with a number of students saying they did not mix with students on other courses. Some students were also less integrated into the groups and were viewed as being 'people who very much keep themselves to themselves' yet, at the same time, one student's perspective on their experience was that 'I didn't know anyone because I live so far away'. Therefore, this indicates that while friendship groupings may be strong, they may not necessarily be socially inclusive. As well, some groups appeared to be divided into those who were keen to persist and those who were less motivated. One student reflected that:

> I think that was quite a big divide in our group. There was a group of us that wanted to get on and do work in every lesson, tried their best to put down the right notes. And then another group that would just be a bit disruptive and just talk and leave it all to the last minute.

In another group, attendance appeared to have been a problem with on occasion, only three students attending out of twenty enrolled on the course, which the students explained as being because 'people dropped out through the year because they couldn't be bothered or they come in whenever they can, when they make time for themselves'. As highlighted by Thomas (2012), a feeling of belonging can involve 'regular contact and the perception that interpersonal relationships have stability, affective concern, and are ongoing' (p. 13) and it would appear that for some students a lack of motivation and difficulties in terms of attendance could pose challenges for social integration, engagement and continuation with their studies.

It was also found that a cluster of the students' comments suggested that the nature of the vocational qualification courses and the associated ways of learning facilitated learner confidence and better peer group relationships, as one student explained:

> I think everyone would agree, like presentations and being more confident, taking yourself out of your shell, talking to new people, I think that helped, because if you're not comfortable and you're shy, coming to a BTEC course kind of opens your eyes a bit more and like you get to talk to other people that you've never met before.

Another student in the same focus group elaborated on this, noting that:

> you have to work with certain people you haven't worked with, I think that's improved like now, I think we do get along, so I speak to people I've never spoken to before.

A slightly different line of thinking was expressed by another student who felt that within A-level groups, students were more competitive and more focused upon grades, and that people who did not get good grades were looked down upon. In comparison, a sense of belonging with peers studying a vocational qualification seems to involve a more level playing field:

> with BTEC it's good because no one looks down on you in any shape or form, you're just an individual that's coming here to study and we're all like engaged in our own life.

In general, the HE students' reflections on their friendship groups at university drew out similar ideas and experiences, regardless of entry qualification and it was frequently said that everybody was initially 'in the same boat' at the beginning of their first-year course. Whilst students seem to most commonly find their closest friends within their particular degree programme of study, they were also conscious of the challenge that large subject cohorts posed to making friends, and that 'when there's 300 people in a lecture theatre it's quite difficult to kind of become close with peers'. This meant that there was a reduced sense of group identity and students within one subject cohort did not necessarily know each other well:

> If I met like hundreds of people, I wouldn't be able to pick out many people and say, 'oh they're on my course', to stop and talk to. I feel like there's two or three people you sit with every time you go to a lecture, but other than that I wouldn't really know who was on my course.

Sometimes the shared subject interest was key to forging friendship groupings:

> the fact that we all have a similar interest which is our course. And we also have an interest in [computer] programming so, you know making friends and having things to talk about hasn't been very difficult.

The HE students with a vocational qualification appeared slightly more likely to talk about forming small friendship groups within their degree subject cohort. A student reflected that 'in Business because it is such a huge, huge course, I think that once you've sort of made friends with someone on the first day that was sort of it, you stuck to your groups and that was it', and another said that 'I just stuck with a couple of friends really'. These friendship groups included supporting each other academically as well as socially, as with this one student who belonged to:

> a really tight group. I think there's only like seven of us and I think it was really good that we all met on the first day because then we were able to do like revision groups and all get together to actually work.

Another student directly contrasted this with their college experience where, 'we were a small group everybody knew everybody really, and it was a lot of my friends'. An A-level student also noted that the sixth form experience of forming relationships was easier compared to that at university:

> You meet a lot of people, and you build like communication through seminar groups. Other than that, there is not a lot in terms of the course because lectures are so big whereas in sixth form, I think, there is a stronger network because your classes are smaller, so it is easier to build networks, rather than university because it is a bigger amount of people, larger in number.

Some of the students with a vocational qualification also felt their friendship networks were influenced by the way others viewed their qualification. One student reflected that 'even with my closest friends, there's always like an ongoing joke about people that did BTECs' whilst another felt 'people judge you and they're like, you've done a BTEC, you're not capable enough to be here'. The comments voiced by these students suggest that the stereotyping around having a vocational qualification could raise potentially damaging psychological issues, particularly in terms of identity and confidence building (see Mountford-Zimdars et al., 2015). However, the students seemed confident about their decision to do a vocational qualification, with one student saying, 'I did it because I knew I wanted to do sport and I absolutely loved doing my BTEC, I learnt so much and I had a great time doing it' and another argued that 'the way I see it is well, we've finished and we're at the same place, like at a good uni to get a good degree'. A different student with a vocational qualification also raised the point that coming to university was also something of a culture shock, indicating that economic, cultural and social capital can also impact upon some students' transitions into university:

> It was a bit of a surprise at how academic people were, and I guess it's more of an income thing as well. So, I'd say probably there are a lot more, I'm probably generalising a little bit, but a lot more middle-class students. So, I guess it was tough to adapt to, but it was definitely worthwhile.

Another vocational student also felt that university required students to become more independent because, for example, you might be:

> picking a module where you don't know any of your friends who are on it. So probably a bit more independent, yeah, and it might be the case you have to go to lectures on your own.

For several A-level students, this was viewed as being an advantage for creating broader, more diverse networks:

> In all our different modules you'll be in a different like presentation, different project group and stuff like that. And I've really enjoyed that because you end up meeting so many really interesting people normally from all over the world.

Another reflected on the way networks can be loose rather than tight friendship groups:

> there's a lot of people I know but I'm not really close with, but they're really nice and you can just sit with them in lectures or get to know them through your tutorials. It's really nice.

Students also commented positively about other ways of learning, including working in small groups, such as in laboratory classes because they had helped to facilitate the formation of social networks. On the other hand, another A-level student found the modular pattern with 'people from different courses doing the same ones' and felt that 'when there's 300 people in a lecture theatre it's quite difficult to kind of become close with peers'. A similar perspective was offered by a student with a vocational qualification, who felt that tutorial groups of twenty were 'quite big' and 'you sit next to someone different every time and they don't want to talk to you, and you don't really want to talk to them'. Some students naturally make friends easily, whereas others struggle more, but students' preparedness, or the nature of groupings at university may need some attention. On one particular degree programme, a residential course was mentioned by two students as having been very helpful in this respect: 'I think that's where a lot of us made most of our friends and we're still friends with them now, the ones we met in [name of place]'. In addition, a vocational student commented that study on a Foundation Course at university helped the formation of a strong friendship group that had carried on to their first-year study on a degree programme:

> we all did foundation year, all played in the [football team], so it's like I'm still with lads who are actually the same age as me, we're all on to our first years now. So, I felt it just gave me a very good understanding of university life.

The establishment of this friendship group was also academically supportive and had also influenced their accommodation choices where these students opted to share accommodation in their first year, an aspect of students' social experiences outlined next.

Accommodation Choices

The interviews and focus groups with first-year Higher Education (HE) students revealed that those who chose to live at home made that decision based on a variety of reasons, such as the financial cost, the comfort of having family support and ease of location. These students, as well as some who lived in accommodation off campus, appeared to have found it at first, slightly harder to participate in the opportunities that university offers in terms of establishing new and broader networks. Students who lived at home recognised this, with a few commenting that they found it initially difficult to establish friendships, as illustrated by this A-level student:

> During the start [of the first-year] it was a lot more [difficult] because of the people who were there the whole day spent more time with each other. Then as the course went on and time went on you see them a large amount of time, so it didn't really make that much of a difference But, during the start, the welcome week and the first few weeks it did, it was a lot more difficult living at home.

Yet on balance, students felt that the benefits of family support outweighed the disadvantages. One student with a vocational qualification reflected that:

> I have missed out on a few things, but at the same time it's really nice just to live at home and just have that comfort as well that support, especially during the examinations.

A different student with a vocational qualification also said, 'I think it's [living at home] made it a lot easier, I don't know what I'd do if I was in student accommodation. I probably wouldn't last two days.' Whilst another vocational student explained that:

> I've spent a lot of time with my family, we're really close as a family so for me when I was choosing my unit was really important for me as a person to find someone close to home as well. So, when I did find out that I got into the university it was really the best thing for me. I think for me, my family when it comes to [university], they do support me quite a lot.

For a very few students though, the opportunities for socialising and establishing new networks became restricted by the need to travel home, as one student with vocational qualifications explained, 'I won't enjoy myself too much, I won't drink because I have to drive home' but also that 'I can't really participate in sports because it is early starts and that means I have to get up 4.00 in the morning, or something'. A small number of students also stated that the cost of living in halls had played a role in their choice to live at home. Overall, it appears that the financial savings were perceived as being worthwhile:

> Obviously weighing up paying for halls here or a ten-minute drive, I just decided to stay home. But the first couple of weeks it was a bit like, oh maybe I should have moved out. Because like the first few lectures people already seemed to know each other and stuff, but like I've made like a close group of friends now and so for me it's not felt much different to moving out.

For some students, establishing social networks was made more challenging by the dominant culture of university life, particularly in relation to drinking and partying, and to attitudes to education. For one student, more emphasis upon educational support would have been helpful:

> I think there could be some other services as well for help, for education help, rather than social stuff. But when we had our Freshers it was mainly going partying and we really didn't need that.

It was evident that some students saw the university as fundamentally about gaining a degree, a view sometimes shaped by parental influence. Two students, who had a vocational plus A-level entry qualifications, who took part in the same focus group and who were ethnic minority students, made comments about this. For example, one student noted:

> my parents have pretty much conditioned me to think that education comes before friends, so in that way I think I don't really need that many friends as long as I've got close friends I can rely on.

The other student said they had made a new friend who, like them, believed, 'education is a higher thing than social life'. One student went on to say that their particular friendship group had decided that 'our education came first' because they had noticed their grades were dropping. They decided not to go to the common room where they got distracted but felt this meant other people stopped asking us completely if we wanted to go to the common room to play some kind of game or do something. So again because of how we are, it's stopped us from making friends. The other student with a vocational qualification (plus A-level) commented that:

> People in uni think they're more into having the party life, while we don't really go out because our parents told us not to go out and I think people would rather be friends with people who want to party because that's what they do. So, because we don't drink or party, they find it difficult to ask us to go out with them.

The comments made in the chapter by these students point to a sense of not fitting in or belonging to certain aspects of a university culture. Such feelings can also be experienced by international students who are living and studying a long way from home. Three international students drew attention to the difficulties of initially feeling homesick at the start of their first year and, as this A-level student said, becoming adjusted to studying in a new country:

> I'm an international student, so it's like you have all of that on your mind and then you have this course that you've never touched before, it's completely different from the way you thought it was going to be.

Another international student reflected on their experience, with comments emphasising again a sense of not feeling socially integrated and thus, alienated:

> I found it pretty hard because my family were living in Dubai at the time so in Freshers' week, well when I was feeling a bit down it was like they were so far away, you felt alienated almost and this was like my first time in the UK.

Taken as a whole, many of the interview comments made about moving into student accommodation or halls provide insights into how this transition is experienced and the ways in which students begin to gain a sense of independence and confidence. One student with a vocational qualification highlighted that living on campus not only made it easier in terms of 'closeness and receiving support' but also the feeling that:

> it does make you more independent because you have to cook for yourself, you've got to do all this [juggling academic and student life] and I do feel more confident because I've had that independence, that exposure.

Students also discussed forming friendship groups outside of their subjects and these took place largely within their accommodation. Some students felt they had built stronger friendship groups through their accommodation arrangements, rather than through their subject groups. One student said that 'the majority of my friends are in my halls' and another explained that 'we're kind of a bit like a community if you know what I mean, so we're all really good friends'. The enjoyment of being in halls was increased for some Sports Science students, where combined accommodation and course worked well:

> it's good that you're in halls for first year, I think that helps. And especially because where we are – we're all Sport Science pretty much. So, you get to know everyone on your course at the same time because you're all in the same area.

One student who did not live on campus in the first-year stated that they had 'found making friends quite difficult' and concluded that 'I would always recommend first years to be in student accommodation, just because it's so much better on campus and [you] automatically make friends like straight away'. One student with a vocational qualification commuted into the university every day for personal reasons, and felt that this had affected their capacity to build a friendship group:

> I feel like during Freshers and things like that I did miss out quite a bit and obviously I probably haven't made as many friends, like flatmates and things like that, but I've still made a few good friends. But I think the commute for me, I'm just tired of driving to and from every day so I've got myself a place with her [names friend] next year, so that'll be –yeah, I think the social aspect of things that's probably what I've missed out on quite a lot.

Indeed, other students recognised that the transition to university 'might have been more difficult for those that lived out, rather than the ones that lived at home'. Therefore, overall it would seem that students who live off campus might experience difficulties forming friendship groups, but there are also key advantages such as the provision of family support and financial benefits.

Extra-curricular Activities

It was also evident that extra-curricular activities were a source of social networks and friendships. Very few FE students talked about their experiences yet one student did explain about how this had helped to extend their social networks:

> they allow the college students to go to the gym, trampolining, ice skating. I used to go ice skating and then you will meet some people that do different courses there.

In HE, it is clear that for the Sports Science students, participating in sporting activities was very important, particularly for students with a vocational qualification. Being part of a sports team was reported as a positive experience, 'the best thing', by everyone who mentioned it. For one student, the sports activity allowed for a more varied friendship network, meaning that they were:

> able to go, right, I'm on my course with my course mates and then I go and have a chat with my team mates and then when I want a break from the team I go back to my course mates.

Another student with a vocational qualification also 'wanted to do as many sports as I could but realised at Freshers that they're all very expensive to sign up to' highlighting that limited finances can impact negatively upon the participation in various activities. This is an important point because many A-level students commented positively about being involved with sports clubs and activities, as this student's comments reveal, illustrating how they can facilitate the creation of friendships:

> I would say try something new as well. So, for me I started scuba diving, I'd only really done it once or twice before and now I'm doing it like every week practicing and it's been really good to meet new people and make really good friends with them because they enjoy what you're doing like you said. And so, take in every opportunity you can.

Students also commented that they got involved with university societies which not only engaged with their personal interests but also helped create a more diverse network of friends. One student reflected that:

> The people that I've met from different courses have been through the societies and through my flatmates so there's no one in my flat who's doing the same course as me and we all have different friends and like we're quite sociable.

Another had joined:

> different societies like sailing and although I'm in 'Women in Business', quite a lot of the girls who are in that society aren't actually doing business management or in the business school, so that's been really nice and I've met some of my closest friends from the societies.

An A-level international student of African origin also discussed how friends had advised joining the African community society, but felt that university was an opportunity 'to learn new cultures, new people, I don't want to go back to the same group of people you know', suggesting a desire to broaden experiences. In the end, however, this student did join the African society because it helped reduce feelings of homesickness:

> you still need to be around like people so you don't feel too homesick, because they're going to be listening to the same type of music you listen, they eat the kind of food you want.

There was a sense in many of these comments that university societies gave students the opportunity to broaden their experiences, both through the society focus and through the wider network of people that it brought students into contact with. Significantly then, the data suggest that vocational students were much less likely to join societies. Only one student with a vocational qualification (plus A-level) mentioned joining a society, although some vocational students recognised that it might be a good thing to do, and one expressed a retrospective regret at not joining any societies:

> there's not much engagement going on between us and people on other courses and I did say to myself I'm going to join societies, but I just never ended up doing it. But I think this year I am planning on joining more societies so I can meet more people.

One student with a vocational qualification (plus A-level) who lived at home observed that they:

> didn't get involved with lots of societies because we have that travelling around, you know events start at maybe 6 but then lectures finish at 12, so there is a lot of travelling around between home and uni.

This comment, therefore, might further indicate how living at home could further influence student life and sense of belonging within the university community.

Conclusion

This chapter has examined a number of themes associated with the social transitions that students might experience at university, as well as in FE. It was found that FE students can build strong relationships with peers and this can be supportive. However, not all groups are equally as strong and inclusive as others. In general, this was also reflected in the first-year HE students' voiced experiences. Central to these transitions is the notion of a sense of belonging and the students with vocational qualifications in this study reported mixed experiences of 'fitting in' during their first year of university. Some had very positive stories, while for others accommodation arrangements, dominant cultures associated with drinking and socialising, larger teaching groups or financial constraints were sometimes cited as reasons why developing friendship groups and social networks was more difficult. In addition, the way that vocational qualifications can sometimes be stereotypically viewed by others can also influence student confidence and sense of belonging. However, such difficulties are not isolated to students with vocational qualifications, for example, students with international qualifications reported feelings of homesickness, alienation and difficulty in adjusting to a university culture in a different country.

For both FE students studying a vocational qualification and first-year university students, it emerged that ways of learning, such as teamworking, oral presentations and smaller class size can have positive effects upon peer relations, friendship groups and building learner confidence. This relates to the work of Goodenow (1993) who proposed that a sense of belonging at school reflects 'the extent to which students feel personally accepted, respected, included, and supported by others in the school social environment' (Goodenow, 1993:80). In turn, this feeling of belonging could facilitate students' motivation and engagement. At the same time, the students' experiences of transition in relation to ways of learning, as discussed in Chapter 4, highlighted different perspectives and different levels of comfort with the more social, rather than individual, ways of learning.

Overall, the student voices reflected here point to social integration and a feeling of belonging being a powerful influence upon students' social transitions. Students bring with them different kinds of social capital and this may be realised in differing degrees of engagement and belonging. The fact that some students (possibly particularly non-traditional entry, including vocational, ethnic minority and international students) may be more likely to form friendship groups with people like themselves suggests they draw on what Putnam (2000) described as bonding capital. In contrast, students who seek to create new networks of friends draw on bridging capital, building relationships across multiple networks. Whilst bonding capital may support a sense of identity and local belonging, it nonetheless disconnects those in the group from the benefits and opportunities that bridging capital may offer. For selective universities which perhaps historically have been less 'open' to non-traditional students, an ongoing commitment to gain a holistic understanding including the educational, social and cultural backgrounds of the whole student cohort should become a central objective, supporting a shift towards more inclusive and equitable student experiences.

There are some strong resonances between the student voices sounded here and in the two previous chapters and some of the conclusions of Mountford-Zimdars et al.'s (2015) literature review of the causes of differential outcomes in HE:

> Curricula and learning, including teaching and assessment practices: Different student groups indicate varying degrees of satisfaction with the HE curricula, and with the user-friendliness of learning, teaching and assessment practices.

> Relationships between staff and students and among students: A sense of 'belonging' emerged as a key determinant of student outcomes.
>
> Social, cultural and economic capital: Recurring differences in how students experience HE, how they network and how they draw on external support were noted. Students' financial situation also affect their student experience and their engagement with learning.
>
> Psychosocial and identity factors: The extent to which students feel supported and encouraged in their daily interactions within their institutions and with staff members was found to be a key variable. Such interactions can both facilitate and limit students' learning and attainment.
>
> Mountford-Zimdars et al. (2015, iii)

In particular, Mountford-Zimdars et al.'s conclusions relating to the user-friendliness of learning, teaching and assessment practices; the quality of staff-student relationships; the importance of a sense of belonging; the differences in how students from different backgrounds draw on differing kinds of social capital; and the nature of support received through within-institution interaction seem to be echoed in the student experiences described in these three chapters. They provide salient pointers to possible action in both FE and HE to reduce the challenges of transition and to reduce the potential for differential outcomes by recognising more proactively the diversity of interests and experiences of the undergraduate community.

References

Baumeister, R. F., & Leary, M. R. (1995). The need to belong: Desire for interpersonal attachments as a fundamental human motivation. *Psychological Bulletin, 117*, 497–529.

Braxton, J. M., Milem, J. F., & Sullivan, A. S. (2000). The influences of active learning on the college student departure process: Toward a revision of Tinto's theory. *The Journal of Higher Education, 71*(5), 569–590.

Goodenow, C. (1993). The psychological sense of school membership among adolescents: Scale development and educational correlates. *Psychology in the Schools, 30*, 70–90.

Jones, R. (2008). *Student retention and success: Research synthesis for the Higher Education Academy*. York: Higher Education Academy. Retrieved from: http://www.heacademy.ac.uk/resources/detail/ourwork/inclusion/wprs/WPRS_retention_synthesis. Accessed on April 14, 2019.

Maestas, R., Vaquera, G. S., & Munoz Zehr, L. (2007). Factors impacting sense of belonging at a hispanic-serving institution. *Journal of Hispanic Higher Education, 6*, 237–256.

Maslow, A. (1968). *Toward a psychology of being*. New York, NY: Van Nostrand Reinhold Company.

Mountford-Zimdars, A., Sabri, D., Moore, J., Sanders, J., Jones, S., & Higham, L. (2015). *Causes of differences in student outcomes*. London: HEFCE.

Putnam, R. D. (2000). *Bowling alone: The collapse and revival of American community*. New York, NY: Simon and Schuster.

Thomas, L. (2012). *Building student engagement and belonging in higher education in a time of change: A summary of the findings and recommendations from the what works? Student Success and Retention Programme*. Retrieved from: https://www.heacademy.ac.uk/system/files/what_works_final_report.pdf. Accessed on March 27, 2019.

Tinto, V. (1998). Colleges as communities: Taking research on student persistence seriously. *The Review of Higher Education, 21*(2), 167–177.

Yorke, M., & Longden, B. (2004). *Retention & student success in higher education*. Bodmin: Open University Press.

Chapter 7

Lecturer Perspectives on Entry Qualifications and How They Affect Student Progress

Helen Lawson

Introduction

In this chapter, we share the perceptions of tutors and lecturers which helped to inform our understanding of the transition from FE college into university. This chapter draws on data from interviews with staff from our HE and FE partner institutions. Eleven interviews were conducted with HE staff at three institutions, and seven interviews were carried out with staff from four FE colleges.

This chapter explores staff views of student performance and progress, academic skills and subject knowledge, academic support, ways of learning and assessment with a focus on perceived differences between students who studied vocational qualifications, and students from an A-level background. The interviews with lecturers uncover sometimes-contradictory viewpoints. On the one hand, there is a general perception that students from a vocational background will struggle and find the transition from college to university trickier than those students who studied A-levels. On the other hand, however, discussions around academic literacy show that most lecturers do not consider there to be a significant difference between students from the different academic qualification backgrounds.

Performance and Progress

HE lecturer responses to questions about student performance and progress seemed to reveal that many of them perceived students with a vocational entry qualification as being more likely to 'struggle' and perform worse during their first year than students with A-levels. As discussed in Chapter 2, progression data from HE to some extent support the assumption that the performance of students with vocational qualifications is not as good as that of A-level students. One lecturer, for instance, observed that they would 'expect' to see a proportion of vocational students 'at the bottom end of the average marks for the year'. The reason for this, they considered, is not:

> [...] necessarily to do with their capability, it might be more to do with the kind of conflict between what they were used to and then the transition and I think it'd probably be fair to say that's probably a relatively common pattern across the business programmes.

The perception that students with vocational quantifications are struggling was echoed by another lecturer from a different institution, who said that 'we've said you can just come in with that BTEC distinction profile and the simple logic about that is we're just setting them up for a fall'. This lecturer explained how, after it was picked up that progression and achievement statistics were dropping, they 'dug more deeply':

> [...] and we saw that quite clearly our pure BTEC students coming in were having about a 10% lower first year experience. A typical A-Level student was high 2:1, to Firsts, BTEC was sometimes 15% lower than that [...] the A-Level experience is flat as far as attainment going through and your BTECs are creeping up over the course of the three years, which is great, but what that's meant is that as a BTEC student you're more likely to graduate with a 2:2 or below. If you come in at A-Level or IB, you're more likely to graduate with a 2:1 or a First. That's not to say that you can't [achieve] and you're destined to follow that pathway [as a BTEC student], but that's been the profile overall.

A similar view was expressed by another lecturer who had discovered that one of their programmes had a particularly high student dropout rate. Between a third and two-thirds of students with vocational qualifications dropped out of their course within the first year, and those students with vocational qualifications that did progress, did so with low credits. The lecturer added:

> It's looking like this year in the programme where we did have a reasonably high percentage of BTEC only students, that those were the ones who have tended to struggle. And I think we will pay more attention to this as time goes on in future years about the progress of particular student groups.

This lecturer's view was that accepting students with BTEC only, D*D*D*, with no requirement for an A-level, 'for some staff that reinforces their existing perceptions, I think, of how BTEC prepares students for university'. These 'existing perceptions' are not altogether positive and, as highlighted in previous chapters, have centred on problematising students with vocational qualifications, rather than regarding systems, processes and attitudes within HE as problematic. In order to increase numbers of students progressing and reduce student dropout rates:

> That programme has now tightened up [...] its entry criteria and in line with some of our other programmes and is requiring an A Level from 2018. So the direction of travel seems to be that the data we do have around progression indicates that BTEC students are struggling [...] And the way that that is being dealt with is to tighten up the entry criteria rather than to provide more support for the students when they're here.

The lecturer commented that requesting a BTEC plus an A-level 'had had some success' but they also considered that it is important:

> To actually talk to them about the fact that they are BTEC students and the fact that that doesn't mean they can't do really well [...] So to motivate them but to make them realise that there are different issues here.

Explicitly identifying students with vocational qualifications carries both risks and benefits. On the benefits side, it can be argued that this approach of overt identification means that students who may need additional support will be alert to this. However, the risks with this approach are that it is underpinned by a deficit discourse and presupposes that all students with vocational qualifications will encounter problems that students with A-levels will not. Moreover, labelling students in this way means that they may think that any 'issues' experienced are due to their academic background alone, and applicable only to them. This approach also assumes not only that appropriate advice and support are in place but also that students will access what is available. As indicated in the preceding chapters, this study has highlighted that it is unhelpful to assume that all students with vocational qualifications will experience particular problems while A-level students will not.

Interviews with FE tutors also highlighted concern about the dominance of the A-level as the route to university, a viewpoint reinforced by the demand for an A-level in addition to, for example, a BTEC 'thus giving the A level again the kind of, key to university'. Against this backdrop, and without the A-level key to open the university door, students studying vocational qualifications often have the perception that university doors are closed to them:

> I don't think a lot of students know at the beginning that with BTEC they can go on and go to university. It's the traditional school, A-level, university, I don't think a lot of the students come into the college with that perspective that they're going to

> go on to university afterwards. [...] they think that the A-level student are the brighter ones, and that they're doing a more vocational route. They don't see it as quite the same value, the same equivalence.

> A lot of the students here do see themselves as being on BTEC is being less than A level, and therefore them not being academically good enough to go to university, particularly when you are doing BTEC because you failed your GCSEs.

> It's often the second alternative, so if you're clever enough you go and do A-levels, but maybe if you're not quite clever enough or you haven't done so well in the examinations, think about BTEC.

In recognition of concerns from FE colleges, coupled with the appreciation of the logistics involved in enabling a student to study both A-levels and a vocational qualification, one HE has amended their admissions criteria for one of their courses so that students no longer need an A-level as well because:

> having talked to local colleges that's just an impossible timetable feat for them. So we've taken that requirement out, so they have just have to have the BTEC and the distinctions across the board.

These comments from some HE lecturers suggest that, at a general level, there are lecturers who have particular expectations and assumptions about the performance and progression of students according to academic background. At the same time, the majority of HE lecturers considered that students with vocational qualifications have the capacity to perform well academically and the potential to succeed so long as students 'take it seriously' and, 'have the right attitude'. One lecturer considered that 'if you get on track in your first year and take it seriously and really want to perform, if you've got some ability which you have if you passed the BTEC, then that can be enough for you to succeed'. They added that it 'impresses' them that 'that some students here are doing very well from a lower starting point'. Indeed one lecturer suggested that 'the differentiator is who's prepared to turn up and knuckle down and just engage. That's the thing'. These are comments that could equally apply to students from any academic background, but many HE lecturers consider that students with vocational qualifications have experienced lower expectations than students with A-level qualifications:

> If you think about the subliminal text that's given to the students when they're 16 about their sixth form choices, we hear all the time that certain students will say they got 'well you're not quite

at A-Level standard so why don't you do the BTEC?' now all of a sudden I mean obviously that pathway you're back in the mix then with those A-Level students and they're sitting next door to you, but inevitably that's going to play on your confidence – am I worthy to be here? Now that takes a bit of time of realising that actually it's up for grabs now.

A perceived lack of confidence in vocational students was mentioned by several lecturers, one of whom commented that he thinks a lot of vocational students feel that HE is 'really for A-level students' and that 'they're almost apologetic' for being at university:

There's a bit of that they've stolen a place at university. And when they get a bit of confidence and realise that they can do it, and a lot of them we see in their second and third year, despite being a disparity in the grades that seems to maintain a little bit throughout, there are BTEC students that fly and go in amongst the A-level students for the top grades.

Another lecturer considered that:

They [vocational students] feel themselves that they're not as good as the A-level students. So the confidence level when they are the start is very different. They have to battle with dealing with information that is fairly new to them in comparison to the A-level students, and feeling not very confident in doing that, which makes the process even harder,

Clearly self-assurance impacts on performance and progress and low self-confidence can act as a barrier to successful academic performance, becoming something 'that inhibits them', creating a 'self-fulfilling prophecy', as one lecturer reflected:

I'm a BTEC student, I did BTECs because x, y, z – that makes me inferior in some way to x, y, z and therefore I'm going to have a problem. So you've actually built in a set of barriers before you get anywhere near university.

Additional comments on student confidence from lecturers included:

We definitely see they've come as a big fish in a smaller pond and they were the triple D student and now all of a sudden they're not. They were getting 80s, 90s and suddenly they're getting 40s and 50s and I think that can be an amazing confidence zapper from that.

All FE tutors talked about managing student expectations and (perceived) misplaced confidence about the kind of university they could succeed at. One FE tutor suggested that:

> It depends on the institution and it also depends on the student that is coming through the FE process and trying to guide them to the right place. What we don't want to do is send them to a university with the wrong expectations and then it go wrong for them. We try and align their skill bases and also what they are interested in doing.

A few FE tutors account for what they see as misplaced confidence in terms of a sense that students from vocational backgrounds do not have a clear understanding of what university entails work-wise, or the support that will be available to them:

> [...] and the nurturing, the support mechanism, they probably won't get as much − you're thrown in, here you go. And I think they like the idea of university but I don't think they understand the work behind it. Yes, the learners at level 3 think going to HE is an easy transition however there are big expectations and this may not be fulfilled.

One FE tutor stated that they try to 'scare' students in the second year:

> We do drum it into them and we talk to them and we invite people to come and tell them what university experience is like, and you know to sort of scare the hell out of them, so they know what it is going to be like and are ready for it.

The general concerns, expressed here, regarding the preparedness of students with vocational qualifications for university, have shaped the support developed by one FE college, which has been designed to better prepare students for university:

> [...] I'm making it stricter [...] no colloquial language, no contractions. So I'm preparing them for the grammatical requirements of university. And that is very interesting because they still write 'don't' and I write 'No you write 'do not'. And it's about getting the team and the teachers on board to say 'Look we're preparing for university. At university they can't use colloquial English, they can't use contractions. It's formal writing.

This college is also considering creating a unit that is 'just lecture based' and:

> see how the students get on with that. And therefore that would be a good reflection of how to deal with university. It's just a possibility for us to think about in the future.

Support currently available includes drop-in sessions run by the library which include essay writing and Harvard referencing, and tutors cover different academic skills in tutorials each week. There is also support provided for students who have not achieved the grades needed in mathematics and English:

> [...] those students that haven't got the grades, is it four or five these days, will be doing resits, so they will be getting extra sessions per week in their English and their maths if needed to do those resits. So they're getting support beyond the Business lessons.

The tendency to regard vocational qualifications as not being 'rigorous enough for students to be able to succeed' was reflected on by an FE tutor who also pointed out the negative language sometimes employed when talking about vocational studies which:

> [...] can be sometimes derogatory by the government, by universities, by institutions, some BTEC students feel that they are not as academically able as other students. Once you have that mentality university is perhaps not seen as an option.

Observations by both FE and HE staff highlight that it is critical to take a far more holistic approach to student progress, and to move towards thinking of students as more than qualifications and grades. As one lecturer pointed out, student background is an important consideration and 'there's a big difference between what grades represent depending on the context of the student'. Consistent with the research discussed in Chapter 2, FE tutors also perceived students with vocational qualifications as potentially having more challenging or disadvantaged backgrounds than students who follow an A-level course:

> I think society today there are a lot of social issues, the majority of my learners, like I said I've got over 100, they're trying to balance home, work, probably looking after brothers and sisters, maybe a carer or they've had financial issues or they're providing for the parents.

Academic Skills and Subject Knowledge

As indicated in the earlier chapter on Ways of Learning, the expectations of academic literacy at university were one area where many students had struggled, and of course, because of the predominance of assessment being conducted through written modes, it may be particularly significant for progression and outcomes. It might be assumed that lecturers would perceive the literacy skills of students from an A-level background as better than those from a vocational background, given that writing is a core feature of more academic qualifications.

However, the interviews with HE lecturers reveal a much more complex picture, and it is not possible to draw a straightforward correlation between students from an A-level background and sound academic literacy, and vocational students and lack of academic literacy.

Some HE lecturers considered that academic essay writing is an area that students with vocational qualifications will struggle with more than students from an A-level background, in particular, 'it's that writing with argument and synthesising an argument they can struggle with at times'. However, other HE lecturers noted that writing is an area that a lot of first-year students find bewildering, and there does not seem to be any consensus between lecturers on whether one particular group of students might find essay writing more or less of a challenge than another group. Indeed a number of lecturers considered that it was not possible to draw a clear-cut distinction between the academic literacy skills of students based on vocational or A-level background alone:

> I couldn't honestly tell you in terms of writing, whether any particular entry profile groups are stronger than the others [...] If for example we get a student with A Levels in physics, chemistry and maths – very good A-Levels, As, A*s, they may still have difficulty with writing essays.

Their perception was that 'different students bring different attributes, different skills' and an observation that, although there may be differences in academic literacy skills between students based on academic background, there may also be differences based on previous learning styles and cultural differences:

> I mean personally if we were talking about accounting and finance students the majority of students come from mainland China so my Chinese students when it comes to numbers are brilliant. They even challenge me. But when it comes to writing or presentations then that's a weakness, but it has nothing to do with their previous entry qualifications [...] So that's a massive challenge, not only I guess for our department but across the business school and university or even the country, because it's difficult to manage that variable particularly in year 1.

An additional issue is that students have to employ 'the whole breadth of skills', regardless of the degree they are studying. Some students might:

> struggle with the writing but are very good at the maths, there are lots of students the other way round [...] there are very few ideal students who have the skills right across the board.

A few lecturers commented that knowing *how* to write is not necessarily the problem. It is knowing *what* to write, understanding how to approach content at university level and 'that you don't just read one paper and write about this paper. You need to read ten papers and come down with what you think'. This may be to do with how students are taught. It is important that students are signposted to the appropriate academic literature and skills in how to engage with it are developed, ensuring students know 'exactly what's being asked of them':

> If you have lectures that are like a spurt of information, without any attempt to show how these things have been linked, how do you expect them [students] to do that [engage with academic literature] without getting some examples of, 'I told you about this and about this and about this, now look at this.' But [...] you have to do that for them. If you don't do that for them they just don't know what it is and how to do it.

Linked to this, several lecturers also find that students find it hard to 'not just memorise pieces of information, but the fact that they need to bring different areas of information together and come up with a single colour from a spectrum', and back up an argument with evidence, quoting appropriate texts. Referencing is one area where most lecturers considered A-level students to be stronger than students from a vocational background:

> [...] rather than referencing a specific point, they think it's okay to go, 'Well, these are my sources and I've just put them in a bibliography at the end.' [...] we get the quote marks they put a quotation like it's an authority, and then that's their end of discussion on that point. And that's not necessarily restricted to BTEC students, but I do notice it a lot in BTEC students.

Of course, there is no requirement in either vocational or A-level courses for referencing to be used, which one lecturer felt 'is not encouraging them enough'. Two HE lecturers comment on the 'Google' generation, and the way in which students now research information. The ability to use the internet for research has 'removed a lot of intermediary steps, through which a student actually learns more about the production of viewpoints of academic material and the like'. Reliance on the internet to conduct research was also commented on by several FE tutors, one of whom also said that 'I can't remember when the last time I've seen a student with a book, a level 3 book. They tend to go straight onto the internet and research. So the back to basic, the root of research, isn't there'.

A difference in subject knowledge between students who had taken subject relevant A-levels and those who had studied vocational qualifications or non-subject relevant A-levels was commented on by some lecturers. For some of lecturers at HE level, vocational students are perceived as having strengths where there is 'practical application' but 'struggle with the really, really academic stuff. They're not as good as the A level students' and find 'dealing with theory' a challenge. A second lecturer teaches 'a complicated first year module' and also considered that if students:

> haven't done chemistry or biology at A level they're going to struggle with it. And obviously if I'm dealing with students that haven't done A levels, I know they definitely haven't done those two A levels [...] I think they're [vocational students] certainly worse prepared, as a rule, for the basic scientific content of the course.

A number of HE lecturers commented on the challenges many students have in terms of their numeracy. The diversity of academic background and students' mathematical skills was discussed by a lecturer who considered that:

> we typically will have say a 50:50 split between those that have done maybe A Level maths or Economics and those that did maybe only maths up until the age of 16. So it's very diverse. Within that then, often you'll get students particularly entering year 1 who are very concerned about the more quantitative elements of the programme and that's quite a strong feature of the programme, in part because it's a BSc but also employers expect those numeracy skills.

One lecturer felt that students with vocational qualifications and students who do not have mathematics A-level may find the mathematics element of a course more challenging than students with mathematics A-level: 'I suppose if they've done straight BTEC they won't have done maths in sixth form', in addition to which 'there are a number of our students who've done maths A-Level and have got an A*, so there's a big difference between the group'. Another lecturer agreed that 'the maths can be an issue' for students but that this is not necessarily an issue for vocational students alone. He pointed out that there is no requirement for students to have 'anything beyond GCSE grade B maths', which means that 'some students really struggle with the quantitative stuff', especially if they 'have taken two, three attempts to get a grade B in maths, they really, really can't do maths and they really, really struggle on that side of things'. For some lecturers, it is specific aspects of the courses that will cause 'less numerate' students problems, such as one course's more technical modules, the quantitative science element of one course and financial accounting on another, for example '[...] there's a particular concept in double entry book keeping, until it's clicked the whole thing is just a struggle and a confusion'.

The difference in students' levels of academic preparedness was viewed as a potential source of difficulty for lecturers in terms of finding an appropriate level at which to pitch the teaching and subject content and getting students 'all up to speed because they come from very different places, so trying to reach a base level'. This means that in the first year 'some of our exceptional students who come in [...] actually find the first year probably fairly straight forward. But other students who maybe just got over the bar to get in find it harder'. Another HE lecturer also described the challenge in pitching the first year module:

> [...] in such a way that is not going to be awfully boring for the good students, but it's not going to awfully overwhelming for the weaker students. It's somewhere in the middle ground, probably skewed towards the weaker end of the scale [...] But at the same time it's not fair for the people who do get three As at A Level for their work to be set at a level that isn't appropriate for them. It makes it more difficult to push the A Level students higher if you know you've got some people in there that are weaker.

Academic Support

Academic support at HE varies within and between institutions. However all the universities interviewed provide academic support and advice to students through, for example, academic development workshops on essay writing, referencing, report writing, use of the different IT packages, presentation skills, 'roving help' provided by maths students, a 'skill sessions around effective reading, what makes a good essay answer' which one lecturer identified as 'a skills gap'. One lecturer listed some of the specific support available: 'sessions on preparing for examinations, supplying students with annotated literature reviews, notetaking (which is something that students particularly struggle with) and peer mentoring'. Another reflected that 'I think before, some students went through the net in terms of those sorts of skills and now I think we're very much targeting that more directly'. There was awareness that support resources such as helpdesks enabled students 'to feel comfortable to ask any question to do with chemistry or understanding of those particular topics that might have come up in my module'. Support is often provided by master's or PhD students who are experienced in a particular area of work, such as statistics, and a lecturer liaises with that person when a piece of work, for example, a lab report, is due:

> So I'll make sure they know exactly what's in there. And I can talk through the types of things that I've told the students already, just to make sure we haven't got a contradictory message. Because that's the worst thing that we can have is I'm

saying to the students, 'These are the types of things I'm looking for in your introduction, methods, results and discussion section.' They go along to the writing desk and they come away confused that they've just been told something different.

There was a recognition that different students bring different challenges and that this may have nothing to do with entry qualifications and has, instead, to do with:

> the nature of the material. It's a different way of thinking and suddenly they are faced with finance which is a completely new module, new style of learning, new style of delivery and therefore we tend to have our own frameworks of support for that.

The support framework for one course at one HE includes targeting students who are deemed at risk at the end of year 1. At the start of the following academic year:

> we have regular one to one meetings with them to alert them and make them aware that look it's important that you catch up with the previous year if you want to progress.

One lecturer commented that even though their academic workshops are voluntary a lot of students sign up to them.

There are significant differences in HE lecturer awareness of student academic background and, subsequently, differening perspectives on whether and how to offer targeted support to students based on prior academic qualification alone. One lecturer talked about how 'on a day to day basis', they were 'probably not aware of that, unless they're my personal tutees'. However, at cohort level he was:

> [...] very aware of it [...] you're very aware of the profile of your intake. So you know their backgrounds, where they've come from, you've got a list of those at the end of the year when you're looking at the programme annual review. You've also got the students' progression rates, success rates based on ethnicity, social background, and entry qualifications around that as well.

Another lecturer voiced an awareness of the potential hazard in distinguishing between students' entry qualifications – 'we don't flag BTEC and A-level students up because that could be seen as setting up problems from the start'. In contrast, one HE lecturer said that he made

> [...] a point of looking that up and trying to find that out and trying to run the programme accordingly and try and provide remedies that might help students accordingly on the basis that

I could see that some of our students, a lot of our student BTECs were struggling and failing.

In some institutions, students who are struggling are picked up through formal mechanisms, which as one lecturer noted, disregards entry route: 'you're not taking any consideration into a student's background at all, you're just looking at absolute performance'. Another lecturer described how they would actively find out a student's academic background if they were tutoring them on a one-to-one basis but 'when I'm teaching them in larger group scenarios or certainly when I'm giving lectures I would have no idea at all and I imagine that might be the case for others'.

In contrast to this, other lecturers made a point of finding out their students' background. In these cases, individual lecturers have developed a variety of methods for finding out who has studied a vocational qualification and so may find certain aspects of a course more of a challenge than students who studied A-levels. This then means lecturers are able to offer or suggest targeted support. For example, one HE lecturer reported a distinct and personal approach to supporting students by telling students within the first couple of lectures that if they have not studied certain A-levels they may find the work 'a bit more tricky'. He described this approach as 'a bit contrived' but:

> it tends to draw people out, I get quite a good mix of people coming down to the front afterwards, and a lot of those tend to say, "I didn't do A-levels, I've done BTEC". And it used to be almost apologetic from people, "I snuck in here on a BTEC," which is ridiculous. But it's a good opportunity, that first point with them, to put their mind at ease a little bit and say, "I did a BTEC." And it's good to tell them that the director of undergraduate studies ... did a BTEC and went on to university, did a PhD. So if you can see them at that point, if they're in any way apologetic at that point and then I tell them that, they're like, "Oh my gosh, we might be able to do this." ... It's instilling a bit of belief in people that they can do it, and it always helps when I tell that that was my background.

Tutor groups are also a way that specific support can be offered. At one HE institution, certain tutors are deliberately assigned students with vocational qualifications 'and they're aware that they're BTEC students and we look for them to just sort of help in a slightly different way' and:

> to recognise early as students come along, to actually talk to them about the fact that they are BTEC students and the fact that that doesn't mean they can't do really, really well.

Some HE lecturers would like to offer targeted support to students with vocational qualifications but are wary of making things worse for a student rather than better by making them feel inferior to other students. Comments included:

> The last thing I want to say is 'okay so you came here with a BTEC, so you're more like to have a few problems, so what's going on'? We have to be more subtle and professional than that, so in short as a personal tutor providing pastoral support through those organised meetings.

One HE lecturer described how he is:

> [...] conscious of walking a tightrope. Of saying "Okay, everyone in the whole cohort, if you're a BTEC student I'm going to need to talk to you afterwards because [...]" I would never do that, I don't think anyone ever does that. But in some ways that would be useful because it's just a targeted approach.

However, the targeted support offered by one HE to students did little to encourage them to actually attend what was on offer. As a result they have built in tests to act as a 'safety net':

> ... We use the success in those academic tests to put them in touch with that support, because we found that when we did it earlier and it was just, "Would you consider – ?" or "In our experience we've found that people with this qualification struggle a little bit more – "then it just falls on deaf ears and no-one turns up. So this has been a way through.

Even with this approach the number of students who take advantage of the support offered is way below the number of students advised to access the support:

> I mean we're literally getting four or five people bothering to turn up when we were asking maybe 30 or 40 to turn up.

In terms of pastoral support, HE lecturers do not have the same level of personal information about a student that FE tutors have. For example, one lecturer talked about the difficulties of providing appropriate support and assistance to students in HE if they do not disclose relevant aspects of their personal situation:

> As a personal tutor, unless they disclose that, you do not know that they have been accessing all of these different types

of support because they are struggling so badly [...] If you then go to an appeal and you haven't got a good reason for saying why didn't I use the university's extenuating circumstances, you'll lose your appeal as well. So those students just get excluded, often just because they were too shy, too nervous, didn't understand what they could do to help themselves.

Students that have studied a vocational qualification at an FE college are likely to have benefitted from a wide variety of support to guide them through their academic work and to address any issues or problems that might hamper student performance. Comments included:

[...] it is an open door situation. I am more than happy to spend time with a student that needs some assistance, or wants to talk about an issue.

The extent of the support available to students at FE is perceived as both 'positive' and 'negative'. The majority of FE tutors acknowledged that students need to be better prepared for university in terms of the reduced pastoral support available to students in HE. As the preceding text illustrates, students receive a lot of one-to-one support, 'I mean we are all over them all the time, helping them out, improving their work', and one FE tutor asked 'is this really a good thing'? because 'when they go to university all that network of support fails to be available, then those students will struggle'. He noted that the 'time set aside for tutorials probably is not anywhere near what they're used to'. For this tutor:

[...] the question that we face is, you know, I want to help you but is helping you hindering you. So, you know and it is a conversation I have with the teachers because what I want to do next year is perhaps decrease the support for some learners, to prepare them for university but then that could jeopardise their success in the college. So it is a tough one.

Lecturer and tutor comments highlight the very different levels of individual support available at FE and HE. Student numbers and the way that vocational qualifications are taught mean that tutor-student input is much higher at FE than HE where, generally speaking, the onus is on the student to understand where gaps in their skills lie and to access the support to address those gaps. There were very different views on the optimum ways to ensure all students acquire the academic skills required to succeed and some lecturers felt that support targeted specifical at students with vocational qualifications was necessary. For the majority of HE lecturers that was a sense of frustration that students do not seek advice and support when they need to, even though they are made of aware of and directed to this support. This aligns with the voiced experiences of the students who often knew where to seek support but were sometimes reluctant to access it.

Ways of Learning

From the interviews, it is evident that lectures and seminars continue to be the 'cornerstone of higher education' and are the dominant ways of learning at HE. All lecturers reported lecturing to large numbers of students at one time, ranging from over 200 up to 400, and so, 'when you're in that size it's pretty hard to do much else'. As the following comments highlight, in the main lecturer perceptions are that students do not enjoy the lecture experience and much prefer small group working. The reasons for this are manifold but centre on student unfamiliarity with lectures as a way of learning which has a strong impact on student participation and engagement.

For one lecturer, it is vocational students who:

> don't know how to learn, just osmosis learning, they think by turning up that's all they need to do. You can sometimes see them in lectures [...] the impression is they're [...] a rabbit stuck in the headlights.

However, on the whole, lecturers felt that, in the first year, all students can find lectures difficult because 'they're not used to what a lecture is'. The lecturer comments here strongly echo the experiences noted by students in their interviews, and suggest that lecturers are aware of the challenge of lectures in the transition year:

> I think all of our students, not necessarily by qualification, struggle with lectures when they get here, they just don't get it. They don't get this idea of basically creating their own set of materials and ideas from their reading and their lectures.
>
> They're sitting in one of the five big lecture theatres we've got, and there's 220, 230 students in there, it's like, 'Wow.' So maybe they get a little lost in that, but it's the nature of the beast.

A further reason suggested by another lecturer for students' dislike of lectures was because:

> [...] more and more we're finding that all our students are wanting to be told, whereas that's not how we work. We pose questions. And sometimes they struggle with that, and certainly that increases throughout the degree.

Picking up on the perception that students feel lost in lectures, a feeling of 'distance' and 'detachment' when teaching a large group was touched on by several lecturers who considered that this can have a negative impact on student participation and subsequently on their performance. In the same way that there was frustration expressed by some lecturers that students do not actively seek support when they need it, there was also frustration that 'students don't actively participate, they don't seem particularly engaged. They've bothered to turn up but they don't engage verbally either with peers or with staff'. Indeed one lecturer observed that 'the biggest challenge I've personally had throughout my time at here is to encourage participation particularly during tutorials'.

In order to stimulate active participation one lecturer talked about how they complemented their 'large class teaching' with seminars and tutorials so that 'students who've come from sixth form [...] feel a bit more confidence to speak or ask questions'. Other lecturers discussed how they will include mini online quizzes in order to help students learn certain aspects of a course, such as muscles and attachments. Even so lecturers reported challenges in securing active engagement:

> [...] you can try to make it as interactive as you can and you can have activities that break up the lecturing. It can be challenging and students, some engage, some don't engage particularly well. I think if you ask students they would probably unanimously say that they prefer smaller group teaching.

Several lecturers perceived reluctance to speak up and participate as being about not feeling comfortable with their peers. Student reticence was not necessarily related to background, nationality or qualifications but because, at the start of their first year, they do not know each other very well and they 'don't want to make themselves look silly': as a consequence, 'to launch into group work or to stand up in front of their peers and give a presentation, that's something that does take time to develop'. Another lecturer also draws attention to 'that social influence' which will affect student participation:

> You don't want to put your hand up and ask the question [...] So that's always one we struggle with, you can run discussions boards or Q&A things electronically, it's getting them even to engage in that is difficult. I don't know whether they feel, 'Oh, I'm going to feel pretty stupid if I do this,' in whichever way, but actually everyone's been through that.

The general perception was thus that students prefer to learn in small groups:

> They don't feel that they can learn best in these circumstances and they are very much less likely to participate. If you ask

> them questions. There will be no answers. I think it's a little bit daunting for them in the first year. They like tutorials so they like smaller classes.

Another lecturer added:

> You just intuitively know, and you see it in their faces, that they get more from the smaller interaction because they're more comfortable to ask questions, in a way it's a safer environment.

For one lecturer, however, engagement can still be problematic even in smaller groups because:

> I think that part of the problem is in tutorials they don't come prepared for it. There is no knowledge, they haven't researched that area, and then they are not brave enough because they don't have anything to say and don't know the subject, and they don't want to feel or look foolish in front of everybody.

In contrast, another lecturer from a different discipline considered vocational students to be stronger than A-level students in terms of their contributions in tutorials because:

> I think a lot of very able A-Level students prefer to keep quiet. Now there are bound to be differences among BTEC students but I think at the better end, at the more confident end, they are very, very good, particularly in my area, where it can be about issues, it can be about their personal experiences, how they experience sport and PE up to that point in their lives.

This perception links very much with the view among HE lecturers that students from a vocational background will perform best on the modules which include practice-based pedagogical approaches. The consensus is that vocational students are 'much better at the practical side of things', feel very comfortable with learning by doing, and 'hands on' methods which include 'interaction', such as coaching and games-based learning to look at theory and practice. One lecturer explained:

> That's where they tend to do really well, on that kind of programme [...] Then on the [Sports Science] programme they have outdoor education which is delivered through some baseline lectures and then they go to Coniston for three days. They go to the [name of centre] and that's a [Sports Science] one, so it's very much hands on, it's totally their environment, they love it.

At one university, there are three sports-based degree programmes from which students can choose and the lecturer 'speculates' that students with a vocational qualification have:

> a leaning towards this programme because a lot of that is applied, it's about interaction. There's a lot of practical based PE type coaching, games-based stuff to look at theory and practice. And that's where they tend to do really well.

However, in modules taken by students from all three programmes, he states that students from the more practice-based programme 'do comparatively worse' and 'score lower' than students from the other two programmes.

In contrast to the dominance in HE of lectures as the key way of learning, FE tutors reported teaching and learning strategies which were more varied and could accommodate individual student learning styles and preferences. Ways of learning on vocational courses might include a '45 minute didactic session [...] and then they are given the opportunity to try it, and so they are learning it through practice and I think that is a really big deal'. Another FE tutor said that they 'tend to try and mix, we try to hit audio, visual and kinaesthetic within every lesson, and also people will try and do individual, pair, and group tasks within every lesson as well'. In one college every student has an individual learning plan, they have information, 'on every student' and they try 'as best we can, within the timeframes and with what is practical, to teach as many different styles for as many different students as possible'. Another tutor's account typifies this group of responses:

> [...] in my class I've got people who really struggle with written work on the board, but video they're brilliant with. So we use a lot of video, a lot of diagrams in the thought process, rather than reading. But how we actually teach really depends on the group.

This perception is borne out by comments from FE tutors who described teaching and learning on their vocational courses as being practical, and aimed at developing students' employability:

> The BTEC is very much vocation orientated and we're thinking about the students in terms of their future working lives and the skills that they're going to need. At A level it's much more academic, much more, I would regard as traditional in terms of delivery, we teach the theory, we use a lot of case studies, we use a lot of report writing, essay writing. But we are focused on the exam and exam preparation. So it's quite different to the BTEC.

For this reason, tutors described learning at FE as drawing on real-life situations, the real world, and, for example, live briefs from businesses so that learning can be applied to non-academic settings. Tutors considered that most students enjoy this way of learning and for the students, 'It is like "Wow!" because it comes to life' and:

> Students seem to enjoy they enjoy discussions and debates, they enjoy what we call simulation activities. We often pretend to be a business [...] so they enjoy that. They enjoy when they get live briefs from companies, because they can actually understand the world of work.

One tutor expressed the view that some students' awareness of the more personalised learning of FE courses, and particularly of the vocational courses, and their knowledge of ways of learning at university may deter some students from considering a university education:

> I have a number of students across my groups who suffer with anxiety, and it really puts them off education. And they are questioning whether to go to university on or not, based on their perception of what university is, and the fact that it may well be a delivery and the examinations as well, rather than the small groups where it's lots of interaction.

Certainly, as was evidenced from the student interviews, the transition from ways of learning in FE to those typical at university, perhaps particularly at the selective universities, does pose some students a challenge.

Assessment

Similar to ways of learning, modes of assessment seem to be another area where HE lecturers perceive significant differences between students with vocational qualifications, and students with more academic-oriented qualifications. Although the interviews with HE lecturers reveal that some courses do include a variety of different assessment methods including coursework, reports, practical classes, case studies, website design and reflective diaries, assessment by exam dominates. Examinations are likely to be a familiar assessment model for students from an A level background while the prior assessment experiences of students with vocational qualifications are markedly different. All FE tutors commented that they were as flexible as possible and employ a wide range of assessment techniques in order to accommodate student assessment preference.

Lecturers raised a number of reasons which influence the difference in approaches to assessment between FE and HE. Some HE lecturers considered that a degree course should be aimed at the higher-achieving students, that it is 'important' for students to be able to write under pressure and that examinations are perceived as being the optimum way to do this. In addition, examinations are deemed to help guard against plagiarism. Moreover, where there are 400 students on a module, examinations and multiple choice question papers (MCQs) are regarded as the only realistic assessment method. Student numbers also mean that the flexibility to assess in ways which students might be more comfortable with is not seen as a viable option by the majority of HE lecturers. Nor is it possible to provide feedback to students on a one-to-one or small group basis, something which is common practice for vocational study, even though some HE lecturers felt that 'learning from feedback is almost the most powerful way of learning'. As one lecturer explained:

> It's a huge group, we're talking about more than 200 students. So small seminars and small group teaching is next to impossible, as is a variety of different formats of assessment. So we assess with multiple choice questions, which suit some students, it doesn't suit other students, but it's only a single way of assessing.

At the same time there was recognition from HE that many students with a vocational qualification background will find writing under pressure 'a difficult challenge'. Some HE lecturers perceived students who have studied vocational qualifications as being less experienced not only in having to do examinations but also in having to prepare for them, compared with students who have studied A-levels, who are used to 'going away, doing revision notes, following old tram lines [...] even when the sun shines'. One lecturer reflected that for students who studied vocational qualifications, not having taken an externally set examination for two years means students may have 'forgotten what strategies they employed when they were doing their GCSEs [...] I think it comes down to confidence as opposed to inability to do it'. Another HE lecturer commented:

> Certainly when you're talking to personal tutees who are BTEC students, they just don't know what they're meant to be doing to get ready for examinations. It's a real struggle. They're used to having this constant diet, a rolling diet of stuff going on all the time [...] We have year one modules which are 100% assessed on end of year examinations [...] I think all the students feel a little bit unsure, but certainly the BTEC students feel most unsure about that.

On the positive side, this is one area where the perceived gap in attainment by exam between students with different qualifications might decrease with the introduction of the revised BTEC programmes which include externally assessed examinations. However, concern and anxiety about examinations were talked about by both FE and HE lecturers. The downside of introducing an element of external assessment by examination is the detrimental impact this may have on students who have deliberately chosen to study vocational qualifications due to what one lecturer perceived to be a 'fear of examinations' and a preference for learning by doing. One FE tutor, for example, talked about the number of students on vocational courses who 'hate examinations, so the BTEC is brilliant for what it stands for and it gives them the opportunity to apply for advanced apprenticeships and university'. As another FE tutor observed, a 'side effect' of introducing more examinations is that 'forcing them through a level II exam now' will be 'very stressful for them' because:

> at the end of the day, if they go into the exam and fail, they have one shot at it. Whereas with the BTEC they have more opportunity to take their time, gather things in.

All FE tutors spoke about the wider support that they are able to provide students:

> [...] we can provide help with understanding of the content we're delivering [...] if they have the right statements in place, we can have extra time, 25% extra time to do that. They have scribes, they can have people to read their work before it's handed in.

Another tutor described how small classes mean that tutors are able to recap all the work done before giving out the assignment brief, and how:

> you can do almost mock tasks in class [...] so students know what is coming, but if people still aren't quite understanding what you've been teaching, you can then take the time and maybe not give the assignment then, change the assignment schedule, put that back and actually revisit it as a group.

One FE tutor noted that tutors 'can't say what they [students] need to put into their assignments' so if students, 'ask how to complete an assignment it's very difficult for us, we're not permitted to tell them how, what to put, and where to put it'. This is slightly at odds with the students' comments where many felt that in FE they were given much clearer direction about what they needed to do in assessments to achieve certain grades − in contrast to their university experiences. However, another tutor expressed the view that there is flexibility within the vocational courses which is not available at A-level so that:

> if people still aren't quite understanding what you've been teaching, you can then take the time and maybe not give the

assignment then, change the assignment schedule, put that back and actually revisit it as a group.

In addition to this, one FE tutor remarked that:

We shouldn't be setting assignments unless we are totally sure that the students have all the information they need to complete an assignment. When we do feedback we can identify where they have not met criteria, but we cannot inform them of what they need to do to put into that to get that area better.

Tutors felt they should be telling students to, 'run, crawl, get there and submit it' but this is not stringently enforced. This FE tutor added that when writing an assignment, students will often ask, 'how many words for me to get a distinction', or if they are three or four points away from 'getting the full grade', they will come to him and say, 'if you let me resubmit I will get it. At university you can't do that'. FE tutors acknowledge that the resubmission option for vocational students:

does not give a clear understanding of what university is like. In the second year of this course, we try to be more stringent and that is part of the process of preparing them so that is the QCF [Qualifications and Credit Framework]. The NQF {National Qualifications Framework] which is a new qualification, has tried to address that by having four examinations.

All tutors who taught vocational qualifications remarked on the ways in which they are as flexible as possible with regard to student assessment, so 'when a student has a particular barrier we will try and support that student to achieve the outcome that they should get that they will', and will 'run any type of assessment that suits the student'. One tutor also considered that students 'respond to that flexibility' and that assessing students in a variety of different ways 'adds a bit of diversity to the course'. For example, one tutor explained that the assessment methods offered for one level 3 Business course were 'as practical as we can make it' and included an assignment for each unit, a presentation, running a meeting, an academic poster, a series of emails or posters. This was not simply about variety in assessment but about a recognition that different assessment modes were better preparation for life beyond school or college:

[...] to demonstrate understanding of a particular topic and the ability to present it in different ways, maybe as a PowerPoint, maybe as a written report, maybe as an email. In other words, typical business documents that they might be asked to produce in the workplace.

In addition, another FE tutor remarked that:

> Because we offer such a variety of assessment students do recognise that there will be some tasks that they won't like, they won't prefer. But there will be other tasks within the same assignment that are more suited to them. And we are very supportive, so when a student has a particular barrier we will try and support that student to achieve the outcome that they should get.

However, many lecturers interviewed felt that the amount of support that vocational students receive is unhelpful and feeds in to a certain amount of 'learned helplessness':

> [...] they've done it as GCSE students successfully so they got onto the BTEC in the first place, but then not having done it for a couple of years and then they're back in, they lose faith and confidence with that. So we do work on reminding them about revision technique, exam technique and the nuts and bolts, so that's not providing an extra hurdle.

Some FE lecturers also considered that the assessment processes for vocational qualifications may not adequately prepare students for the predominantly exam-based assessment methods at HE, 'the shock of a deadline', and the lack of a resubmission opportunity (although university programmes often do have resubmission opportunities in particular circumstances, and/or condonable fails). As a consequence, one tutor suggested that assessment practice in vocational qualifications 'perhaps does not prepare learners for the kind of rigorousness of university'. Nevertheless, the majority of FE tutors felt that assessment methods complemented the vocational nature of, for example, BTECs. Tutor comments included, 'It's vocational so they're going to be doing presentations, they get assessed officiating, get assessed coaching in the gym, so it's a very vocational qualification', and 'a lot of BTEC students that are much more confident with approaching their practical sessions' such as laboratory work. The majority of FE tutors also believed that students 'tend to do quite well in presentations, rather than the written classic essay style'. This perception that vocational students perform best when there is a practical element to their learning and assessment was a recurrent theme. These tutors considered that it is the combination of practical application and individual support that is most effective in ensuring assessment processes are positive and constructive for vocational students:

> These students quite often need quite a lot of TLC. They need a lot of group work, and help communicating with each other, and they get lots of that if they come through this route.

We try and nurture them, I think is the right word, where they have the right support. So if somebody really hates presenting, we'll get them to present but maybe in front of the tutor instead of in front of the whole group initially, to build up their confidence, because we don't want to put them off completely. If there's work to be done then obviously we'll liaise with learning coaches to discuss strategies of how we can help them and I'm very upfront with my learners – 'What can I do to help you? How can we turn this around?' And they'll probably give me suggestions as well and we try and meet halfway.

A lot of the assignment work, the assessment work is case study based. It's based on real businesses or real scenarios that they're expected to keep up to date with and demonstrate understanding. There is underlying theory, theory in accounts, theory in motivation, in all the sub-business topics there is a little bit of academic study there. But very quickly it's applied [...] And we'll use case studies that we'll look at in the classroom. We'll then move on to do role plays, the students will be asked to do investigative work and do presentations back to the group, so developing their presentation skills as well. It's as practical as we can make it.

The wider experience of assessment methods that vocational students have experienced 'bar examinations' was mentioned by some HE lecturers. Students who have studied vocational qualifications were considered to be 'much more confident with approaching their practical sessions [...] practical laboratory work', and 'they do embrace the coursework early on'. One HE lecturer speculated that familiarity with different assessment modes can sometimes play to the advantage of students from a vocational background:

I think some of the very high achievers don't like doing group work, they'll just depend on their own devices because that's worked. Others may value group work and the contribution others may make to bring up the end product to the best it can be. the type of experience that BTEC students get in schools and colleges, that they like the group work, they like the presentations, they like coming up with a product or some more vocationally oriented type of assignment. Whereas the A-Level students may be more happy or more comfortable with writing essays and sitting examinations.

Thus, although degree courses may include a variety of ways to assess students, lecturer perspectives indicated that the prevalence of examinations as the principal method of assessment is daunting for students with vocational qualifications, many of whom choose a vocational course precisely because assessment is coursework and practice-based. Equally, both lecturers and tutors felt that there is less flexibility at university in selecting assessment methods, in contrast to FE where tutors will 'run any type of assessment that suits the student'.

Conclusion

There is a high degree of correlation between the perspectives offered here by the FE tutors and HE lecturers, and those expressed by the students themselves. The HE lecturers, in general, are sympathetic to the needs of students with vocational entry qualifications, and believe them to be capable of achieving at university. At the same time, they are aware that sometimes students with vocational qualifications do not progress in the same way as those with A-level entry qualifications, and that they face particular challenges. The principal difference between the students and the HE lecturers, and to a lesser extent the FE tutors, is that the lecturers and tutors are more inclined to make binary judgements about the two groups, whereas the student perspectives reveal the situation to be much more nuanced and complex, with students across qualification groups often experiencing similar problems.

For example, one area where both lecturers and students perceive there to be a particular challenge for students with vocational qualifications is in the different nature of assessment at HE. A strong theme in responses from the FE tutors was their adoption of a wide range of assessment options and they offered 'an unbelievable list of types or assessment' designed to complement the vocational nature of these course. FE tutors also reported that the choice of assessment methods is accompanied by considerable individual support. Indeed, there is a strong sense from FE colleges that they will do all that they possibly can to enable students to achieve and progress. For the students themselves, assessment emerged as a significant concern for them once at university, but the divisions reported by the lecturers between students with vocational entry qualifications and those with A-levels was much less clear. The student interviews do suggest that familiar assessment experiences are, as one might expect, less challenging than unfamiliar ones, but examinations can be a challenge even for students whose prior experience included examinations. In general, coursework is a more preferred mode – though there is a diverse range of preferences in terms of types of coursework. The student interviews also offer the reminder that A-levels are less homogenous in terms of assessment than binary distinctions recognise: A-level subjects with highly discursive, written modes of assessment, such as History and English, are very different from the more problem-based assessment of mathematics, or the more practical assessments used in Drama or Art, for example. Similarly, the tutors and lecturers view that academic support is stronger on vocational courses which is not fully matched by the students' experiences. Instead, it seems that FE is much more likely to offer strong support for assessment, with more test preparation, more explicit marking criteria and more direct attention to how to achieve the next grade than the students experience at university. This, of course, is likely to be highly influenced by the high-stakes accountability culture in which FE colleges find themselves, and the institutional pressures to secure successful results.

Very similar conclusions could be drawn concerning ways of learning, where again the students communicated a complex and nuanced picture of their experiences, with differences not strongly aligned to qualification route, in contrast to lecturers' perspectives which drew sharper distinctions. One consequence of these more binary perceptions of the university lecturers, and the differential outcomes of vocational students, is that it may lead to changes in entry requirements which militate against wider participation. Some of the participating universities addressed the differential outcome 'problem' by changing their entry requirements so that students will no longer be accepted without an A-level. In contrast, one university has amended their entry requirements, by removing A-level as a condition of entry, and now asks for Distinctions at BTEC. It is important to note that apparently straightforward decisions about entry requirements which rule out vocational qualifications risk closing a pathway to university for significant, and increasing, numbers of students. And, as noted in Chapters 2 and 3, vocational students are more likely to have the characteristics of widening participation of students. At the same time, whilst national data are revealing differential outcomes for widening participation groups, and in some datasets, for students with vocational qualifications, it remains the case that the significant majority of students in these groups *do* succeed at university, including at selective universities.

Taking the student and tutor/lecturer interviews as a parallel set of insights, what is striking is the synergy between them in terms of their perceptions of what constitutes the key barriers and constraints to progress and outcomes. But what is also very evident is their divergence in revealing a tendency in tutors and lecturers to see different qualification routes in more binary ways, underpinned by a sense that these groups are homogenous, in contrast to the student responses which signal the heterogeneity and diversity of these groups.

Chapter 8

Recommendations for Policy and Practice

Helen Lawson

In this book, thus far, the review of research, the reporting of statistical analyses of student progress through university and the experiences and perspectives of students and teachers in both FE and HE have generated a rich and complex understanding of the needs and experiences of students as they access and progress through university. Whilst the focus has been on students with vocational entry qualifications, many of the insights have been a reminder that the distinctions between students groups are less clear-cut. The student body is a heterogeneous grouping of people who come from diverse backgrounds having had different experiences, but who will share a desire for their time at university to be as successful as possible. Success is not only about achieving a degree at the end of three years (though, of course, this is important!) but also about developing as a person, meeting new people, experiencing new things and making the most of opportunities available. Very few of the issues related to transition are simply about having a vocational entry qualification; almost all issues identified were present in all groups interviewed, although to varying degrees. This underlines that the student body is diverse and there are risks in treating any one group as homogenous. It is important to think about each student as an individual, rather than boxing students into particular groups. In this chapter, we consider some of the key findings from the Transforming Transitions project and what the implications are for policy and practice.

Helping Students to Develop a Sense of Belonging

It is critical for students to feel a sense of belonging and inclusion at university in order to reduce student dropout rates and enable all students to achieve success. As outlined in Chapter 6, the experiences of students with vocational qualifications in this study reported mixed experiences of 'fitting in' during their first year of university. For some, the experience was positive, but for others there were certain elements of university life which made it more challenging for a sense of belonging to be developed. Some students with vocational qualifications commented that their peers sometimes viewed their qualification as something lesser than A-levels or the IB, making them feel that they did not belong in a university. The situation was also true for the international students in our project, regardless of background: they felt a heightened sense of difference and did not always feel they were party of the university community.

A sense of belonging was also generated or disrupted by accommodation arrangements and ways of socialising, which tend to revolve around drinking and partying. Students who lived at home reported finding it harder to make new friends and to participate in the broader aspects of university life and networks, something which was also talked about by HE lecturers who perceive live at home students as much less likely to participate in clubs, societies or internships. Not being able to participate in volunteering, networking opportunities and internships potentially has a long term negative impact on students and their employability. Social capital comes into play here on a number of levels and different students will have different access to different amounts and quality of capital on which to draw. Students with social capital are more likely to be advantaged in that they are more likely to live at university more likely to have had parents that attended university and so will have a level of awareness about university life and the importance of participating in networking, volunteering and internships, and more likely to have the financial capacity to take advantage of opportunities which stand them in good stead when applying for jobs. However, although students who live at home highlighted particular challenges they encountered by not living on campus, they also talked about the positive impact of being able to go home to their families at the end of the day. Living at home not only helped financially, but allowed for a familial network of emotional support. Parental and family influence can also have a significant impact on student behaviour and motivations, and, for some, parents reinforced the view that university is about learning and studying, not about drinking and socialising. These positive aspects of living at home were not recognised or acknowledged by HE lecturers. Instead, their comments reflected a negative perspective and regarded lack of participation in extra-curricular opportunities as being detrimental to the university experience. There is a strong theme evident here of universities tending to have a dominant culture, well-aligned to the needs and interests of a dominant student group, but less suited to the broader diversity of other student groups.

Recommendations

Universities need to ensure that they recognise the potential benefits that students gain from living at home, not simply possible disadvantages. It is important that HEIs actively consider how to support students to develop broader networks whilst at university, enabling them to benefit from opportunities and extra-curricular activities. This might include being mindful of the timing of events so they are easier to join, even for students who travel.

Many universities are already alert to the possible risks of alcohol indulgence, inherent in Freshers or Induction Week. It would be wise to look more broadly at student experience across the university year and to ensure that any dominant culture of drinking and partying is moderated through the availability of different forms of networking and socialising. This may mean looking at Student Unions and how representative they are of the diversity of the student body, and how actively they promote a range of ways of including students from any background.

Student Academic Support

The interviews with first-year undergraduate students show that many students find the nature of support on transition from FE to HE to be markedly different, and sometimes challenging. Many students struggled with the expectations of academic literacy at university. In some cases, it may be that students with vocational qualifications are more likely to find certain aspects of a course more problematic than students who have studied A-levels, for example, essay writing. But it is also important to bear in mind that different A-levels themselves offer different degrees of preparation for academic writing. Reading and understanding of academic texts, and managing wider reading, was a problematic area for many students, as was synthesising relevant information, and referencing appropriately. Similarly, students whose courses required numeracy skills reported feelings of poor preparedness, but this was linked to whether they had studied mathematics post-16, rather than entry qualification. There are some degree courses where it seemed to be advantageous to have studied certain A-levels rather than a vocational qualification. For example, A-level Biology and Chemistry were regarded as being helpful to students studying Sports Science, and some students without A-level Economics reported that they struggled with the Economics module of a Business Studies degree. However, even studying certain A-levels for particular courses was no guarantee that there would not be any gaps in student knowledge during their first year.

What this again highlights is the diversity of the student body and the challenge for lecturers in teaching a group of students who may have very different starting points. Some students may need support, both academic and emotional, in order to make the most of their university life. This involves developing a culture of enablement, by not only ensuring that support structures are in place, both academic and pastoral, but also making sure students know what support they might need, and what support is available to them. Equally important is to highlight to students the benefits of accessing support and to stress that it is ok to seek support, that this is all part of the learning process. It is important to note that there is no 'one size fits all' approach that can be taken to academic support. Moreover, there is no common approach to whether HE lecturers are either made aware, or make themselves aware, of student academic background. Some lecturers will have an awareness of the mix of students at cohort level, but not of individual students unless they are identified as struggling. In contrast some lecturers will make a point of finding out about their students' backgrounds and will offer suggestions to individuals about which elements of the course they may find more challenging, and ways in which this can be addressed.

An added challenge is that our research revealed that students were often aware of the support that is available to them, but did not access it, sometimes due to 'laziness' but sometimes due to feeling 'scared' or 'silly'. Help from their peers, both informal and structured, was found to be an important source of support for students and buddy or mentor schemes were also mentioned by a number of students. Some HE lecturers talked about their frustrations in knowing that particular students should take advantage of, for example, learning support, but also knowing that there is little they can do if a student does not want to engage with support. There were also perceptions among HE lecturers and tutors that students with vocational qualifications receive far more personal and one-to-one support than, for example, students with A-levels. This was reflected in comments made by a number of first-year students who had studied vocational qualifications who felt that the lack of a personalised support and weak relationships with HE tutors created added challenges to settling in and doing well academically. For many students, including A-level students, the support from FE tutors was significant in easing them through their post-16 courses, although not all students felt positively about the support they received, with a few students remarking that the quality of the relationship and support from their tutor was subjective and dependent on whether the tutor and student got on at a personal level. In contrast, many students found the relationship for university tutors to be more distanced and less constructive.

As outlined in Chapters 4 and 5, the differences in approaches to student support could be attributed to the teaching context and the greater academic independence required for a university, while FE, particularly with the high-stakes accountability to examination results, may be tending towards greater dependency of students on tutor support.

Recommendations

As the issues here strongly relate to differences between FE and HE, there needs to be closer collaboration and discussion across the two sectors to ensure that expectations are clear. This might include a formal grouping to include representation from FE, HE and examination boards to agree common expectations in key areas so that students either receive more appropriate preparation during FE programmes, or it is more systematically provided in year 1 at university. For example, concerns about academic writing were raised by both students and HE lecturers. Here there needs to be a clear shared definition of what academic writing is, as it is term widely used but poorly understood, and to what extent it should be part of every FE qualification. This is an important discussion, as the assumption cannot simply be that academic writing must be addressed in FE. Rather, FE and HE need to discuss what is relevant and appropriate to address in each stage.

Whilst universities generally have well-developed academic and well-being support systems in place, students are not always aware of how to access them, and some students are reluctant to draw on these support systems. There needs to be more consideration of how to make these support systems more visible for access, but also how to encourage a culture amongst students where students are willing to seek and use available support. Many universities have academic mentoring structures in place and these may be a useful point of contact for active discussion of support needed and checking students know where to find that support.

Ways of Teaching and Learning

Although there are shifts in the way the notion of inclusivity is understood and defined, the Transforming Transitions project has found that there remains an expectation for students to fit into the ways of being and doing of the university, rather than universities adapting policies and practices to better fit a diverse student body. Traditional forms of teaching and assessment may dominate which means that students from a vocational background are not always given the opportunity to demonstrate learning in alternative ways. This is also true of A-level students from more practical degree subjects, such as Drama, another reminder of the heterogeneity of the student body.

Large group lectures continue to be the dominant way of teaching at university, and this was the most commonly mentioned learning challenge for HE students, regardless of prior qualifications. Some students commented, for example, that the large group sizes and one way flow of information created a sense of detachment from both the group and lecture content rather than a sense of belonging and engagement gained through small teaching groups experienced at A-level and BTEC where it is also much easier to ask for help or clarification. Student comments are reflected in remarks made by HE lecturers who perceive students as feeling lost and distant, and lecturers also feel frustrated that students do not actively participate. However, this may not be related to qualification background but because students are in an unfamiliar setting, surrounded by people that they do not know very well. While some lecturers feel that, given the large numbers of students they have to teach, lectures are the only realistic option, and there is not the flexibility to adapt ways of learning to individual student needs or preferences, there is recognition that students prefer to learn in small groups. There is also a perception among HE lecturers that students with vocational qualifications are much more adept at learning by doing and practice-based tasks, such as coaching and games based learning to look at theory and practice. Similarly, positive comments from students about lectures were related to the delivery style of lecturers, particularly where lectures were made more interactive.

Students who had studied vocational qualifications in particular remarked on the diverse ways of learning that they had experienced in FE which included group work and presentations, and FE teachers also talked about the variety of teaching methods they employ and the importance of finding ways of teaching and learning which suit individual student needs. Awareness of individual needs and adaptation of teaching practices was referred to very little by the university lecturers.

Our research highlights, then, that if universities are to address the learning needs of a diverse student community, consideration needs to be given to inclusive pedagogies. The challenge lies, in part, in bringing about a shift in the view that many hold, that lectures are the only viable option for teaching at university. There is a parallel need for lecturers to develop their awareness of students with vocational qualifications, and to include students' vocational experiences as part of their learning and teaching. Recognition of the strengths and diverse experiences of students with different backgrounds would also help to build student confidence. Many HE lecturers felt that students with vocational qualifications do have the potential to succeed but lack confidence and feel a sense of unworthiness.

Recommendations

The lecture, seminar and tutorial are perhaps the archetypal characteristics of learning at university, but there is an urgent need now to broaden the repertoire of learning experiences to reflect changes in understanding how we learn, and to ensure learning in university is better aligned with best practice in the school/FE sector, and with the expectations of the workplace. A richer repertoire of learning experiences not only benefits a broader group of students, but also challenges those who are very comfortable with traditional ways of working. Learning how to work constructively in a group task to achieve a particular learning goal, for example, is as valuable a way of learning as attending a lecture. Likewise, participating in a seminar discussion which is genuinely dialogic and participatory is as valuable as writing an academic argument in an essay. The lecture is perhaps the iconic representation of university learning, but was surprisingly problematic for students, regardless of background. A way forward here may be to more proactively consider how lectures are delivered in the first year of university, making sure that students understand how to make notes, and that pace and coverage of content are particularly carefully managed (and more obviously, that lecturers are more consistently high quality!).

In a similar vein, universities need to prioritise the development of inclusive pedagogies, drawing on existing best practice in the sector, which argues that inclusive learning and teaching represents:

> the ways in which pedagogy, curriculum, and assessment are designed and delivered to engage students in learning that is meaningful, relevant and accessible to all. It embraces a view that diversity stems from individual differences that can enrich the lives and learning of others. (Thomas & May, 2010, p. 9)

Crucially, inclusive pedagogies focus on the capacity to learn and on being a learner, and reject notions of fixed intelligence quotients (IQ). Instead, deterministic ideas of fixed IQ are replaced by a view of 'growth mindsets' (Dweck,

2012), which are predicated on the idea that we are capable of achieving more than we think we can, if we have the right attitude and an appropriate learning climate.

Assessment Models

As indicated in Chapter 5, the dominant form of student assessment is by examination. Our research revealed that HE lecturers perceived students who had studied vocational qualifications as being less experienced in both preparing for and sitting examinations, where the ability to write under pressure within a set time is all important. Assessment processes can be a concern for prospective university students, particularly where, for example, students chose to study vocational qualifications precisely because of the variety of assessment methods available. Indeed, first-year HE students expressed a strong preference for coursework rather than examinations, and students with vocational qualifications were more likely to be in this group. It is important, however, to note that this view was shared by a significant number of A-level students too. FE tutors also remarked on the ways in which they were as flexible as possible with assessment, employing assessment methods that suit the individual student. All FE tutors were mindful of the fact that students who choose to study vocational qualifications may struggle with examinations, they may have had negative experiences of examination taking at GCSE and are likely to have chosen a vocational qualification where assessment is by a variety of methods through which they can demonstrate their learning. Smaller classes mean that tutors are able to go over work covered and make sure that students understand what is required of them before handing out an assignment, and often they receive stronger guidance on what they need to do to achieve particular grades.

Despite the high level of support for assessment available to students in FE, some FE tutors acknowledged that the transition for students from a lot of support to less support can be extremely demanding. For some FE tutors, there was a voiced concern that the assessment processes for vocational qualifications do not adequately prepare students for the predominantly examination-based assessment methods at HE. There were also concerns that the resubmission opportunity for vocational qualifications does not prepare students for meeting submission deadlines at HE. The provision of feedback was another key area where there were significant differences between the student experience at HE and FE. The amount and quality of feedback on written work in HE meant that many students found it hard to learn from feedback to inform future work, and many students reported that they missed the one-to-one feedback that they had received at FE. The research highlighted that some HE lecturers are very aware that some vocational students in particular would appreciate tailored feedback on their coursework, rather than generic feedback, but they felt that student numbers mean this is not a viable option at university.

Recommendations

In line with the recommendations around ways of learning, one clear recommendation here relates to encouraging universities to adopt a broader range of assessment types, which are better suited to the diverse student community and enable students to demonstrate learning through methods that draw on their differing strengths. This would help bring about a shift in discourse, moving from deficit discourses and stereotyping of students with vocational qualifications to inclusive discourses which recognise the strengths of diversity. This may not mean that students are able to choose assessment types, though this could be considered, but rather that all students have to demonstrate their learning in a variety of ways. It is equally important that students uncomfortable with presentation or group work as a mode of assessment build the presentation skills and collaboration skills needed for these assessment modes, as it is for other students to develop the skills of revision and time management for coping with examinations.

The transition issues related to feedback clearly need to be addressed but require a different kind of solution. Whilst at face value, the obvious recommendation might be that universities should strengthen and develop the feedback they give to students, the problem appears to be more around what feedback is for and what the expectations are. The high-stakes accountability system of the school and FE sector means that feedback on assessment is strongly geared towards examination success, not necessarily towards learning, or developing independence. A critical aspect of a university education is being an independent, self-managing learner, and feedback is often geared more towards learning and future development than how to get a first class degree. This dissonance in the purposes of assessment is the issue which needs to be addressed, and as with core academic expectations, it would benefit from discussion across the HE/FE boundaries and at policy level to agree and develop a more natural progression from FE assessment feedback into HE assessment feedback.

HE Partnerships between HE and FE

Central to the Transforming Transitions project was a collaboration of institutions across the FE/HE divide, and the gleaning of insights from students and teachers in both sectors has proved particularly fruitful. HE/FE partnerships have the potential to support the transformation of student transitions. However, there is currently little shared working across the FE/HE boundary which risks negatively impacting on the students' transition experiences. It is noteworthy that two of the recommendations noted earlier relate to stronger collaboration across the transition. As vocational qualifications are now being acknowledged as contributing to widening HE access (Kelly, 2017), it might be the case that a more collaborative approach between higher education providers and FE colleges can support the progression of these students, and indeed all students, better.

Recommendation

Building closer links between FE and HE would allow for greater shared understanding to be developed. Such collaborations could be both local and national. At a local level, FE/HE partnerships would build stronger relationships and understanding between the two sectors, and would create opportunities for possible cross-sector teaching or shared events. As many students do not go to their local university (although this number is increasing), a local partnership would not be dealing with transition between the two partners but in better understanding of how each sector operates.

However, to mobilise the kind of systemic change that is needed to allow all students to flourish at university, we would recommend the establishment of a national HE/FE forum, supported at the highest level, and including representatives from both examination boards and well-being services, as well as FE and HE staff. Such a body should have the responsibility for addressing some of the key barriers and constraints we have identified, and eschew the very natural tendency to assume the problem should be handled better in the other sector.

Conclusion

Overall, our recommendations are flagging a need for systemic culture change in both FE and HE which more proactively acknowledges and addresses the

Table 1. A Taxonomy of Student Diversity.

Diversity Dimensions	Examples
Educational	Level/type of entry qualifications; skills; ability; knowledge; educational experience; life and work experience; learning approaches
Dispositional	Identity; self-esteem; confidence; motivations; aspirations; expectations; preferences; attitudes; assumptions; beliefs; emotional intelligence; learning styles; perspectives; interests; self-awareness; gender; sexuality
Circumstantial	Age; disability; paid/voluntary employment; caring responsibilities; geographical location; access to IT and transport services; flexibility; time available; financial background and means; marital status
Cultural	Language; values; cultural capita; religion and belief; country of origin/residence; ethnicity/race; social background

Source: Thomas and May (2010, p. 5).

diversity of the student population, and recognises that it is unwise to draw binary distinctions *between* qualification routes, as there are inevitably variations *within* qualification routes as well. Our work has focused on qualification differences; there is often a focus on differences in gender, ethnicity, disability and socio-economic background; however, diversity encompasses a broad panoply of human differences which students bring to their study. One way to illustrate this diversity is represented in Table 1.

Such diversity does require a cultural shift in thinking away from an expectation that students need to adapt to the dominant and preferred way of operating a university to a more inclusive approach, which:

> necessitates a shift away from supporting specific student groups through a discrete set of policies or time-bound interventions, towards equity considerations being embedded within all functions of the institution and treated as an ongoing process of quality enhancement. Making a shift of such magnitude requires cultural and systemic change at both the policy and practice levels. (May & Bridger, 2010, p. 6)

References

Dweck, C. S. (2012). *Mindset: The new psychology of success*. London: Constable & Robinson.

Kelly, S. (2017). Reforming BTECs: Applied General qualifications as a route to higher education. *HEPI Report 94*, HEPI. Retrieved from http://www.hepi.ac.uk/wp-content/uploads/2017/02/Hepi_Reforming-BTECs-Report-94-09_02_17-Web.pdf. Accessed on September 22, 2018.

May, H., & Bridger, K. (2010). *Developing and embedding inclusive policy and practice in higher education*. York: The Higher Education Academy.

Thomas, L., & May, H. (2010). *Inclusive learning and teaching in higher education*. York: The Higher Education Academy.

Chapter 9

Conclusion

Mital Kinderkhedia

In 2016, the Social Mobility Commission published a report (Social Mobility Commission, 2016) which argued that our post-16 education was 'stuck in the past', and which drew attention to two key factors deeply relevant to this book: firstly, that access to selecting universities to students from low-income backgrounds remained restricted, and secondly, that our current system made it 'particularly difficult for lower-income youngsters to translate their attainment at school into qualifications that are well rewarded in the labour market' (SMC, 2016, p. ix). UCAS data (2015, p. 6) indicated that selecting universities were less likely to recruit BTEC students than those with traditional qualifications. At the same time, contemporaneous research was highlighting differential outcomes for BTEC students as they progress through university. In terms of final outcomes, A-level students were more likely to achieve a first than vocational students (Bailey & Bekhradnia, 2007; Gill & Vidal Rodeiro, 2014), and students taking the BTEC Award and Diploma had a significantly lower probability of a first or at least an upper second than students taking an Applied A-level (Shields & Masardo, 2015). Evidence also suggested that BTEC students were more likely to drop out of university when compared with those on a traditional academic pathway, even when accounting for prior attainment (Hayward & Hoelscher, 2011). BTEC students in Russell Group universities were less likely to complete than those elsewhere; the salary gap between BTEC students and traditional students, although narrowing, was significant and at its largest in Russell Groups universities. This emerging pattern of differential outcomes stood in the face of evidence which suggested that young people with more access to programmes and activities which, for example, include work experience, career talks and workplace visits were equipped with better networks, better knowledge of the labour market and made more informed decisions leading to a more successful transition to adult employment (OECD, 2010; Symonds, Schwartz, & Ferguson, 2011).

This body of research suggested therefore that the educational trajectories of BTEC students through university were less successful than those of traditional students, particularly in selective, research-intensive universities. The reasons for this were less clear, particularly since many of the studies were quantitative analyses which rely on outcome data. As a group, BTEC students' differential outcomes have often been overlooked in favour of more dominant discourses surrounding the outcomes for socially disadvantaged students, BAME students or students with special needs. Yet, BTEC cohorts represent some of the intersectionality of factors which can contribute to differential outcomes. As we note in Chapter 2, they are more likely to be from areas with low participation in higher education and demographic groups associated with lower outcomes (Shields & Masardo, 2015); they are more likely to be male; and ethnic minority students are more likely than their white counterparts to have vocational qualifications (Bhattacharyya, Ison, & Blair, 2003). The KCL/HEFCE report (Mountford-Zimdars et al., 2015, p. 96) notes that:

> HEFCE should consider further analysis of the progression of some groups whose outcomes have not been mapped in detail, as well as more research to understand the intersectionality of different student characteristics and their link with progression and attainment outcomes.

Indeed, Shields and Masardo (2015, p. 6) recommended that:

> students with vocational qualifications should be added to the demographic groups for which BIS monitors retention and success. BIS and the Office for Fair Access (OFFA) should consider including students with vocational qualifications in their monitoring and reporting.

It was this backdrop that saw the genesis of this book.

The Transforming Transitions project, which informs this book, set out to foreground and give voice to the particular needs and trajectories of university students with vocational qualifications. At the same time, we were conscious that in examining inequalities for vocational students, we would also be addressing inequalities for other minority groups.

Throughout the book, we have sought to avoid deficit discourses around vocational qualifications, and particularly those deficit discourses which locate problems of access, progress and outcome in the student, not in the system they inhabit. As Devlin et al. noted:

> it can be seductive to think that if non-traditional students are clever enough, or try hard enough, or persevere enough, or believe enough in their own ability, they can engineer their success at university. (Devlin, Kift, Nelson, Smith, & McKay, 2012, p. 1)

This view, that any student can succeed if they try hard enough, ignores the barriers to success which some students face – economic barriers, social barriers and educational barriers. Instead, we argue that there is need to think more creatively about how both Further Education and Higher Education can accommodate the different needs and acknowledge the different strengths of a diverse student body.

In the book, we highlight that in the context of national concern about barriers to accessing the advantages that a university education can offer, which has focused largely on minority groups, insufficient attention has been paid to the impact of entry qualification, not only on university access but also on success at university. But at the same time, we show that entry qualifications may be only part of the story of educational trajectories through university, as they can be a proxy for social disadvantage, and we argue that an overemphasis on entry qualification may increase the existing barriers to access for minority groups. Crucially, we need to think more critically about recognising the benefits of a diverse university community and consider how to make universities more genuinely inclusive learning communities. This will require systemic culture change in both further and higher education – the goal is not to provide further support which aligns non-traditional students with the traditional cohort as this is likely to reproduce current inequalities. Rather, it will need a re-imagining of what it means to be a learner, with consequent re-visioning of teaching and learning practices, and assessment practices – immersed in a culture which welcomes and embraces diversity at its core. Such a re-imagining would constitute what BIesta calls a learning democracy, where education enables:

> the empowerment and emancipation of individuals so that they become able to live their lives with others in more democratic, just and inclusive ways – which, again, is not only important for the well-being of individuals but for the quality of democratic life itself as well. (Biesta, 2006, p. 173)

References

Bailey, N., & Bekhradnia, B. (2007). *The academic experience and outcomes of students with vocational level 3 qualifications*. Oxford: HEPI.

Bhattacharyya, G., Ison, L., & Blair, M. (2003). *Minority ethnic attainment and participation in education and training: The evidence*. Nottingham: DfES Publications.

Biesta, G. J. J. (2006). What's the point of lifelong learning if lifelong learning has no point? On the democratic deficit of policies for lifelong learning. *European Educational Research Journal*, 5(3–4), 169–180.

Devlin, M., Kift, S., Nelson, L., Smith, L., & McKay, J. (2012). *Effective teaching and support of students from low socio-economic backgrounds: Practical advice for institutional policy makers and leaders*. Sydney: Australian Government Office for Learning and Teaching.

Gill, T., & Vidal Rodeiro, C. L. (2014). Predictive validity of level 3 qualifications: Extended Project, Cambridge Pre-U, International Baccalaureate, BTEC Diploma. Cambridge Assessment Research Report, Cambridge Assessment, Cambridge, UK.

Hayward, G., & Hoelscher, M. (2011). The use of large-scale administrative data sets to monitor progression from vocational education and training into higher education in the UK: Possibilities and methodological challenges. *Research in Comparative and International Education*, 6(3), 316–329.

Mountford-Zimdars, A., Sabri, D., Moore, J., Sanders, J., Jones, S., & Higham, L. (2015). *Causes of differences in student outcomes*. London: HEFCE.

OECD. (2010). Innovative SMEs and entrepreneurship for job creation and growth. *OECD Working Part on SMEs and Entrepreneurship (WPSMEE)*. Retrieved from www.oecd.org/cfe/smes/46404350.pdf

Shields, R., & Masardo, A. (2015). *Changing patterns in vocational entry qualifications, student support and outcomes in undergraduate degree programmes*. London: HEA.

Social Mobility Commission. (2016). *State of the nation 2016: Social mobility in Great Britain*. London: Social Mobility Commission.

Symonds, W. C., Schwartz, R., & Ferguson, R. F. (2011). *Pathways to prosperity: Meeting the challenge of preparing young Americans for the 21st century*. Cambridge, MA: Pathways to Prosperity Project, Harvard University Graduate School of Education.

UCAS. (2015). End of cycle 2015 data resources: DR2_033_06 applicants by BTEC. Retrieved from https://www.ucas.com/sites/default/files/app_level_report_2015-dr2_033_06.pdf

Glossary

A-levels	Advanced level – a subject-based qualification conferred as part of the General Certificate of Education – is a school leaving qualification offered by various examination boards in the United Kingdom.
Acceptance	An applicant who, at the end of the cycle, has accepted an admission offer and has been placed for entry into higher education.
Acceptance rate	The number of acceptances divided by the number of applicants.
Age	The analysis uses country-specific age definitions that align with the cut-off points for school and college cohorts in the different administrations of the UK. For England and Wales, age is defined on 31 August, for Northern Ireland on 1 July, and for Scotland on 28 February the following year. Defining age in this way matches the assignment of children to school cohorts.
Applicant	A person who has made an application via Universities and Colleges Admissions Service (UCAS).
AQA	This organisation is responsible for the overseeing of examinations performed in Wales, Northern Ireland and England. AQA is thus the examination board in these countries and stands for Assessment and Qualifications Alliance. For more details, see https://www.aqa.org.uk
BTEC	Originally Business and Technician Education Council, BTECs are qualifications now offered by Pearson.
DfE	Department for Education.
Domicile	Declared area of permanent residence.
Entry rate	Number of acceptances from a UCAS application cycle divided by the estimated base population.
FE	Further Education.
GCSE	General Certificate of Secondary Education.
HE	Higher Education.
HESA	Higher Education Statistics Agency.
IB	International Baccalaureate Diploma.

Glossary

NQF National Qualifications Framework.

OCR OCR (Oxford, Cambridge and RSA Examinations) is an examination board that sets examinations and awards qualifications (including GCSEs and A-levels) for learners of all ages at school, college, in work or through part-time learning programmes. For more details, see www.ocr.org.uk

Offer Provider decision to grant a place to an applicant. May be subject to the applicant satisfying academic and/or other criteria.

Provider A higher education provider – a university or college.

QCF Qualifications and Credit Framework.

Tariff Band Provider tariff bands are based on the average levels of attainment of their UK 18-year-old acceptances. There are three tariff bands: lower tariff, middle tariff and higher tariff. Each group of providers accounts for around a third of all UK 18-year-old acceptances in recent cycles.

T level These two-year technical programmes for young people aged 16 to 19 aim to prepare students for entry into skilled employment, or higher-level technical study. The first three T levels will be available at selected colleges and schools (providers) across England in September 2020.

UCAS Universities and Colleges Application System.

UK United Kingdom. Excludes the Channel Islands and the Isle of Man.

VQ Vocational qualification.

Index

Academic literacy, 60–64, 116
Academic preparedness, 117–121
Academic results, 22–26
Academic support, 70–74, 126–130, 141–143
  recommendations for, 142–143
Accommodation choices, 101–104
Addressing Barriers to Student Success, 6–7
A-level students, 14, 15, 16, 17, 18, 21–22, 23–25, 27, 32, 40, 41–42, 44–45, 53, 59, 73, 76, 91, 93, 111, 133, 139–140, 145, 149
  academic literacy, 60, 61, 62–64
  academic support, 70–71, 120, 121, 142
  adapting to changed assessment expectations, 85–86
  accommodation choices, 99, 100, 101
  assessment preferences, 80–81
  changes in assessment experiences, 81–82, 84
  extra-curricular activities, 102, 103
  literacy and subject knowledge, 116, 117, 118, 119
  modes of assessment, 129, 130, 132–133
  numeracy, mathematics and statistics, 64, 65, 66
  performance and progress, 111–114, 116
  sense of belonging, 141
  social networks, 97, 98, 99
  subject and content knowledge, 67, 68–69
  ways of learning, 126, 127, 128, 143
  ways of teaching, 143
Assessment and Evaluation in Higher Education, 79–80
Assessment feedback, 86–91
  good practice, 92
  helpfulness of, 91–92
Assessment models, 145–146
  recommendations for, 146
Assessment preferences, 80–81
Australia
  differential access and participation, in higher education, 17

BAME. *See* Black Asian and Minority Ethnic (BAME) students
BEC. *See* Business Education Councils (BEC)
Behavioural competence, 46
BIS. *See* Department for Business for Innovation and Skills (BIS)
Black Asian and Minority Ethnic (BAME) students, 23, 149–150
  differential access and participation, in higher education, 18
BTEC, 2–3, 5–7, 9–10, 20–21, 32, 40, 41, 42, 48, 54–55, 133, 143, 149–150

156 Index

assessment preferences, 80
degree outcomes, 50
disparity between institutions granting access to, 19
employment, 27
Extended Diploma, 2, 3
inferiority, 16, 17
modes of assessment, 130, 132
National Diplomas, 15
parity between different qualifications, 54
patterns of progression, 51–54
performance and progress, 113–114
progression and academic results, 21–22, 23, 24–25, 30
qualifications, 14, 15, 17, 19, 25
undergraduate courses, 48–50
Buddy schemes, 70–71
Business Education Council (BEC), 2–3

Changes in assessment experiences, 81–84
Choice, vocational qualifications by, 45–46
City and Guilds of the London Institute for the Advancement of Technical Education, 2
Content knowledge, 67–70
Cycle Report (2016), 18

Degree outcomes, 50, 51
Department for Business for Innovation and Skills (BIS), 54, 149–150
Department for Education (DfE), 39, 44

Destination of Leavers in Higher Education (DLHE), 50–51, 52–53
DfE. *See* Department for Education (DfE)
Differential access, in higher education, 17–22
DLHE. *See* Destination of Leavers in Higher Education (DLHE)

Educational attainment, 17, 40
Educational preferences, 44
Employment, 26–29
England. *See* United Kingdom (UK)
EPQ. *See* Extended Project Qualification (EPQ)
EQF. *See* European Qualifications Framework (EQF)
European Qualifications Framework (EQF), 2
Exeter College, 7
Extended Project Qualification (EPQ), 24, 25
Extra-curricular activities, 104–106

FE. *See* Further Education (FE)
FEC. *See* Further Education Colleges (FEC)
Force, vocational qualifications by, 45–46
Formative assessment, 79–80
France, 1–2
Free School Meals, 18
Further Education (FE), 20–21, 32, 103, 139, 141, 144, 145, 146
 academic support, 142
 social networks, 96–97

tutor perspectives on entry
qualifications, 132–133
academic support, 122–123
modes of assessment, 128,
129, 130, 131, 132
student performance and
progress, 113–114, 115,
116
ways of learning, 122, 126,
128
ways of teaching and learning,
143–144
Further Education Colleges
(FEC), 5

GCSEs. *See* General Certificate of
Secondary Education
(GCSEs)
General Certificate of Secondary
Education (GCSEs),
39–40, 42, 43–44,
66–67, 73, 84–85, 144
Germany, 2
value of vocational education, 16

Habitus, 28–29
institutional habitus, 28–29
vocational habitus, 46
HCEC. *See* House of Commons
Education Committee
(HCEC)
HEFCE. *See* Office for Students
HE/FE partnerships, 146–147
recommendations for, 147
HEIs. *See* Higher Educational
Institutions (HEIs)
HEPI, 49–50
Hereford Sixth Form College, 7
Her Majesty's Revenue and
Customs data (HMRC),
27

HESA. *See* Higher Education
Statistics Agency
(HESA)
Higher Educational Institutions
(HEIs), 15, 18, 29, 46,
140
Higher Education Statistics
Agency (HESA), 18, 20,
21–22, 27, 39, 41–42
degree outcomes, 50
patterns of progression, 50–51
undergraduate courses, 48–49
HMRC. *See* Her Majesty's
Revenue and Customs
data (HMRC)
House of Commons Education
Committee (HCEC), 93

IB. *See* International
Baccalaureate (IB)
ICT. *See* Information
Communication and
Technology (ICT)
ILR. *See* Individualised Learner
Record (ILR)
Inclusion, 139–140
Individualised Learner Record
(ILR), 27
Inequality, 41
Inferior alternative qualifications,
15
Information Communication and
Technology (ICT),
66–67
Institutional habitus, 28–29
International Baccalaureate (IB),
25, 40, 80, 81–82,
139–140
Islington College, 7

JACS. *See* Joint Academic Coding
System (JACS)

Joint Academic Coding System (JACS), 48–49
Juvos, 27

KCL/HEFCE report, 149–150

Labour Force Survey, 26
Labour Market System, 27
Learner identity, student choices and, 29–32
Learning democracy, 150
Learning experiences across FE–HE transition, 59
  academic literacy, 60–64
  academic support, 70–74
  different ways of learning, 75–77
  numeracy, mathematics and statistics, 64–67
  subject and content knowledge, 67–70
Learning in vocational education, 46
Lecturer perspectives on entry qualifications, 111
  academic preparedness, 117–121
  academic support, 126–130
  literacy and subject knowledge, 121–126
  modes of assessment, 136–137
  student performance and progress, 111–117
  ways of learning, 130–136
Literacy, 121–126
Loughborough College, 7
Loughborough University, 7

Mathematics, 64–67
Modes of assessment, 136–137

National Benefit Database, 27
National Pupil Database (NPD), 27
National Strategy for Access and Student Success in Higher Education, 54
National Student Survey, 79–80
Netherlands, the, 1–2
NPD. *See* National Pupil Database (NPD)
Numeracy, 64–67

OECD. *See* Organisation for Economic Co-operation and Development (OECD)
OFFA. *See* Office for Fair Access (OFFA)
Office for Fair Access (OFFA), 149–150
Office for Students (OfS), 5, 21, 22, 23, 25, 28, 30, 40, 41, 49–50, 53, 54
  Addressing Barriers to Student Success, 6–7
OfS. *See* Office for Students (OfS)
Organisation for Economic Co-operation and Development (OECD), 1

Parity between different qualifications, 54
Participation in higher education, 17–22
Participation Of Local AReas (POLAR), 41
Passports to Progress, 18
Patterns of progression, 50–54
Peer mentoring, 70–71
Peer support, 70–71
POLAR. *See* Participation Of Local AReas terminology, abbreviated (POLAR)

Index   159

Policy and practice
 recommendations, 139
 assessment models, 145–146
 HE/FE partnerships, 146–147
 sense of belonging, development
   of, 139–141
 student academic support,
   141–143
 ways of teaching and learning,
   143–145
Post-16 qualifications, 13–14,
   20–21, 24, 149
Prior education, 42
Prior qualification, undergraduate
   admission patterns by,
   46–48
Progression, 22–26
 patterns of, 50–54
Providence, vocational
   qualifications by, 45–46

Queen Mary University of
   London, 7

Regulated Qualifications
   Framework (RQF),
   2, 3, 4
Review of Post-18 Education and
   Funding (the Augar
   Review), 4, 5
RQF. *See* Regulated
   Qualifications
   Framework (RQF)
Russell Group, 7, 17, 18, 20,
   21–22, 25, 30, 32, 47,
   48, 149

Schools' Enquiry Commission, 2
Select Committee on Public
   Accounts, 21
Sense of belonging, 28
 development of, 139–141

 facilitating, 95
 accommodation choices,
   101–104
 extra-curricular activities,
   104–106
 social networks, 96–101
 recommendations for, 140–141
SMC. *See* Social Mobility
   Commission (SMC)
Social capital, 28, 42
Social identity, student choices
   and, 29–32
Social Market Foundation, 18
Social Mobility Commission
   (SMC), 13, 27
 report 2016, 18, 20–21, 149
 report 2019, 54
Socio-genomics, 42–43
Statistical analysis of national
   datasets, 39
 degree outcomes, 50, 51
 parity between different
   qualifications, 54
 patterns of progression, 50–54
 social context, 40–43
 undergraduate admission
   patterns, by prior
   qualification, 46–48
 undergraduate subject areas,
   48–50
 university, 48
 vocational qualifications, by
   choice, force or
   providence, 45–46
 vocational route, 43–45
Statistics, 64–67
Student body, 139
Student choices, and social and
   learner identity, 29–32
Student performance and
   progress, 111–117

Subject knowledge, 67–70, 121–126
Summative assessment, 79–80

Teaching and learning experiences across FE–HE transition, 79
　adapting to changed assessment expectations, 84–86
　assessment feedback, 86–91
　assessment preferences, 80–81
　changes in assessment experiences, 81–84
TEC. *See* Technical Education Councils (TEC)
Technical Education Council (TEC), 2–3
Terminology, problems of, 14–15
Training in vocational education, 46
Transforming Transitions project, 5–9, 14, 49, 50, 142–143, 146, 150

UCAS. *See* Universities and Colleges Admissions Service (UCAS)
Undergraduate admission patterns, by prior qualification, 46–48
Undergraduate subject areas, 48–50
United Kingdom (UK)
　differential access and participation, in higher education, 17
　Higher Educational Institutions, 29
　longitudinal data analysis, 40
　mass expansion of Higher Education in, 13–14
　patterns of progression, 50–51
　post-16 qualifications, 13
　undergraduate admission patterns by prior qualification, 46, 47
　value of vocational education, 16
United States
　differential access and participation, in higher education, 17
Universities and Colleges Admissions Service (UCAS), 3, 5, 14, 17, 18, 32, 46, 48–49, 54–55, 149
　tariff, 23–24, 25
University of Birmingham, 7
University of Exeter, 7

Value of vocational qualifications, 15–17
VET. *See* Vocational Education and Training (VET)
Vocational Education and Training (VET), 1–4, 7, 9–10, 18
　definition of, 1–2
　development of, 3
Vocational habitus, 39–40, 46
Vocational route, 39–40, 43–45, 47–48

Ways of learning, 75–77, 130–136, 143–145
　recommendations for, 144–145
Ways of teaching, 143–145
　recommendations for, 144–145
Wolf Report (2011), 3–4, 15, 16
Working class students, 45

www.ingramcontent.com/pod-product-compliance
Ingram Content Group UK Ltd.
Pitfield, Milton Keynes, MK11 3LW, UK
UKHW021635230326
11407UKWH00015B/32